Jesus' Apostles
True Born Again Doctrine

Clarke Smith

Cadmus Publishing
www.cadmuspublishing.com

Copyright © 2023 Clarke Smith

Published by Cadmus Publishing
www.cadmuspublishing.com
Port Angeles, WA

ISBN: 978-1-63751-372-9

All rights reserved. Copyright under Berne Copyright Convention, Universal Copyright Convention, and Pan-American Copyright Convention. No part of this book may be reproduced, stored in a retrieval system, or transmitted in any form, or by any means, electronic, mechanical, photocopying, recording or otherwise, without prior permission of the author.

I dedicate this book to all the big Preachers on T.V. I have been blessed by their T.V. shows and wonderful books, since I was a youth, they really know the Scriptures well. Sadly I drifted away from Church when I was a teenager. The Preacher didn't want to let my friend in Church, I didn't understand why, till my mother said, that Preacher was racist. I thought Jesus loved us all, like the song, Jesus loves all the Children of the World, red, yellow, black and white, they are precious in his sight. Now I'm thankful that God fixed my heart and mind as He did in Psalm 51:1-17 'Oh how he fix and blots out all sins and iniquities, back on the Cross. Jesus the same yesterday, today and forever. I know how King David felt. Slowly, as we finish these far off days in time, before the coming of the Lord Jesus on the clouds, as we now have the knowledge to reach all nations the Gospel, as Apostle Peter spoke in Acts 2:38-42, then Apostle Paul spoke in Acts 13:46, 47 a light to the Gentiles, that thou shouldst be for salvation unto the (end of the world.) Praise the Lord Jesus, you Big T.V. Preachers can now preach the Holy Ghost, since you received that Holy Ghost, speaking in tongues, the same way as Acts 1,2 all filled with the Holy Ghost fire. As Apostle Paul said in, speaking about tongues, stir up the Gift of Tongues.

I also want to dedicate this book to my little sister, Joyce (Queen Ann) Smith, thanks to you and our Nephews, Jerry and Billy (Wayne O) Smith, Jesus has carried us all through the foot print of sand, in our journey together in this old world.

And a special dedication to all those men and women in prison who was snared in life, by that, liar and deceiver, the old devil. Whom, soon, is Jesus going to destroy him, forever. Hang on brothers and sisters, it's just a short while longer.

From Brother Clarke

Table of Contents

Chapter 1: Saul to Apostle Paul 1
Chapter 2: John the Baptist was Elijah 10
Chapter 3: Horseshoe Games 17
Chapter 4: God's Hidden Treasures, Gold, Silver, Polished . . 23
Chapter 5: Moses' Books to John's Revelation Book 29
Chapter 6: God's First Blood Sacrifice to God's Last Sacrifice . 37
Chapter 7: Fool's Gold 43
Chapter 8: Diamond or Fake 49
Chapter 9: Counterfeit Money 57
Chapter 10: Forerunners 62
Chapter 11: Jesus' Powerful Authority 67
Chapter 12: In the New Jerusalem 74
Chapter 13: Those Who Rejected the True Doctrine 79
Chapter 14: Eternal Life Insurance 85
Chapter 15: Big T.V.'s Holy Ghost Filled Preachers 92
Chapter 16: Fire, After Water 99
Conclusion 104

Chapter 1

Saul to Apostle Paul

As we read this man's journey through history and life. He thought he was doing good for God's kingdom. The big persecutor of Jesus' First Apostolic Church, that started on Pentecost Day, in Acts 2:42. And they continued steadfastly in the Apostle's Doctrine and fellowship, and in breaking of bread, and in prayers. In Acts 7:58 And cast him out of the city, and stoned him; and the witnesses laid down their clothes at a young man's feet, whose name was Saul. 8:1 And Saul was consenting unto his death, and at that time there was a great persecution against the church which was at Jerusalem; and they were all scattered abroad throughout the regions of Judea and Samaria, except the Apostles. 8:3 As for Saul, he made havoc of the church, entering into every house, and hauling men and women, committed them to prison. As we read Saul's persecution, destroying, Jesus' First Church. 9:1 and Saul, yet breathing out threatenings and slaughter against the disciples of the Lord, went unto the High Priest. Saul was devoted. You know the rest of this story. He thought he was doing right. Just like many preacher do this day in far off end times. God used Apostle Paul, to turn this dark world to light. So please don't think, I'm trying to take nothing away from you great Preachers, men or women, Jesus wants to use each one of you, he prepared you all, by giving you the Holy Ghost. God, knows just how much you all are loved and respected. So now, He can use you to reach these far off end times church. You should be proud that he chose you, just like he chose Saul. Look how Apostle Paul finished building Jesus' Church, oh how blessed we all are, to be chosen, for this great Battle, End times. Jesus is ready, are each of you, willing to fight those devils and demons. Those Apostles already built the foundation for us, so let's finish.

As of now, I'm stuck in this prison, I just made (minimum security). If I had a lawyer, I'd be on the streets by now, I have so many different reasons to be left out early release, home detention, or programs or early Parole, God knows the future, His plans, not our understandings. God has all power, just like Apostle Peter's early release from Prison. Well so much about those thoughts, let's get to our place in time. When God's time, has finish me form these prison walls, I shall go to all places, bringing the gospel to those lost me and women, in our far off end time, I don't want to be a Preacher, I've preached many times in Church Prison, I really love to teach the lost, not Preach to the already saved, they don't need my help. Just like in Early Churches, they went town to town, city to city, they wanted all to hear the Jesus built true Salvation way.

The Book of Acts, explains the Early church History, those Early Church Christians, all fought the fight to their final end. Once Paul came out of Darkness to the Light, just like all who gets the Holy Ghost filling, we have to stir up the Holy Ghost filling. Jesus, wants us to bring, all, out of Satan's dark kingdom. Old devil and demons, truly fear Jesus' name baptism, remission of our (sins). Oh the Holy Ghost filling power, you know the Book of Acts. God has given us, the Holy Ghost to bring those men and women, to Saint Peter's Pearly Gates, it's time to lay our hands on them, help all get the promise, like Early Church Saints to us all a far off end times church. If you need the words of (ACTS), search the Scriptures, get hungry. I've broke the Scripture down, so you don't have to look very hard or far. Apostles wrote most of the New Testament – NT - from prison walls. God uses, whosoever He wills, we all are born sinners, till we get out of darkness, into Jesus' saving light, born again of water and Spirit. John 3:5 the old true saying, better late than never, Amen and Amen.

God's ways are different than ours, he blinded Saul, then opened his eyes from darkness, then changed his name to Apostle Paul. Light of the world, Jesus is the light of this world, it's strange how he blinded Saul with that light, now he brings us all out of the darkness, into His light, the old devil has us all in chains of darkness. Adam to last man or woman, we are born in darkness of this world. Call it (sin) or (darkness) or (death), till Jesus brings us into light, removed our (sins) in Jesus' name baptism, then fills us with Holy Ghost, Life. Just like the flood washed all sin away, then the Tower of Babel, God confounded their language, they couldn't understand each other's speech. Then on Pentecost Day, He left them speak in tongues, so all nations, the Holy Ghost power, left all understand, what new thing was about to happen. The Bible tells us, in Proverbs 3:5 Trust in the Lord with all thine heart; and lean not unto thine own understanding. Right, ok, yes. Let us go to Numbers 22:27, 28. And when the ass saw the Angel of the lord, she fell down under Balaam, and Balaam's anger was kindled and he smote the ass with a staff. And the Lord opened the mouth of the ass, and said unto Balaam, what have I done unto thee, that thou hast smitten me these three times? As we read on in these story, we see how the ass warned the man from death, that angel would have killed him with a sword. God is using me (ass) (or donkey) as I once was in Life, to warn everybody, about sin, which can only be washed away, by Jesus' lovely name in Baptism, water. No one wants the second death, that is coming on the Lost, Eternal life into the Light, from darkness to light, let's break those chains, choose now, which place, you and family, friends and Church members, will spend Eternal. Those Apostles and Jesus, gave up their lives, for you and me, get in the water like all the rest of the 3,000 souls did on Pentecostal Day, plus the men and women those Apostles rebaptized and helped them receive the Holy Ghost spoke in tongues. These Apostolic Churches today, still do things, like Saint Peter, said. Just think, only once more in Jesus' name, not like the Old Testament, man. II Kings 5:1-27 that man went down 7 times, he didn't like it, but he did it. Work out your own salvation with fear and trembling, just like Apostle Paul did.

Today we see so much knowledge, information or fact is this world. T.V., Radio, Newspapers, Books, these things helps us in our life and times. As of now, the Book of Revelation, can now be fulfilled, to all the world, to see, at one time, how those two Prophets shall be killed, and then arise in 3 days. I truly don't want to be left behind to see this thing, I want to be with the Lord, not thinking about these hard times, that are about to happen, soon. The kingdom of God is in my thoughts, I'm not focused on this world no more, only for God's lost sheep, I'm trying to reach as many as I can, for Jesus. I don't know the future, but, I do know He is one day soon coming. Who should be caught up in the air, this man, is trying to say, get ready, for you are about to be in Heaven or Hell, Preachers Preach the Jesus' built church of the True Apostle's Doctrine, Acts 2:38-42. Call other Preachers, who has the Holy Ghost gift, don't wait, time isn't our friend, Jesus warned us, tomorrow isn't promised to you. Don't let these far off men and women and family, miss Eternal life. Love them, as Jesus loves us all, like the Prophets and Apostles, all did. Tick, tock, wake up time, hear the warning signs of time, Oh I wish I could reach everybody's hearts and ears, your voice and books, can reach so many millions now, more than 3,000 on that Pentecostal Day.

Jesus, Jesus, Jesus, like the movie Beetlejuice, Beetlejuice, Beetlejuice. Call on Jesus, get the Holy Ghost gift of tongues, born of the Spirit, and water. Yes, get down in the water, in Jesus' name, what can wash away my sins nothing but the Blood of Jesus, not, Trinity dip in water, so if you have questions ask Apostolic True Church Preachers or those other Doctrine, hid the Holy Ghost, share your perfect gift with others, don't kept it hidden, let the Light shine to all men. Blow your trumpet, let those far off end times men and women, go towards those Saint Peter's Pearly Gates, wide open to us all, why the Lord may be found, hear His Voice, come out of those chains of darkness, enter into my light, my kingdom, shine your light, for all these far off End times sheep. Amen. Amen.

Chapter -1- Questions – End

Mark (T) for true of (F) for False

1.) – Chapter -8- Was Saul (Paul) a great persecutor of the Original church?

2.) – Chapter -9- Did Saul (Paul) ask who art thou, Lord?

3.) – Chapter -9- Was (Paul) talking to Jesus, within the light from Heaven?

4.) – Chapter -9- Was Jesus saying that (Saul) was to be a chosen vessel to the Gentiles?

5.) – Chapter -11- In 13:43-52 Did Saul (Paul) tell the Jews that he was set to be a light to the Gentiles unto Salvation?

6.) – Chapter -10- 18-33 Was Paul casting out spirits in Jesus name?

7.) – Chapter -19- 1-6 Did Paul baptize them from John's baptism, in to Jesus' name baptism?

8.) – Chapter -19- 1-6 When Paul laid his hands upon them, did the Holy Ghost come on them when they spoke in tongues?

9.) – Chapter -19- 11-17 Was God working special miracles by the hands of Paul?

10.) – Chapter -26- 1-18 Then Paul try to turn King Agrippa from the darkness and power of Satan, unto God?

11.) – Chapter -26- 26-29 Did Apostle Paul tell King Agrippa, that he also knoweth of these things?

12.) – Paul, said to King Agrippa, I know thou believest thou prophets?

13.) – Did Apostle Paul follow the Acts 2:38-42 Original Church Doctrine that Apostle Peter said, was for them, their children and for all a far off?

14.) – In the Book of Acts, was Paul filled with the same Holy Ghost gift, as that 120 plus 3,000 souls, after he was baptized in Jesus' name and then had hands laid upon him, as he spoke in tongues?

15.) – Did Apostle Paul say in Romans 1:16 – the gospel of Christ is power?

16.) – If Christ Jesus be in you, (Spirit), will your bodies, be raised in Rapture?

17.) – Did Apostle Paul say in 1 Corinthians 14:18 that they spoke in tongues more than ye all?

Song – I Am Redeemed

I Am redeemed (convert) bought with a price, Jesus has changed my whole life, if anybody ask just who I am, tell them I am redeemed. I'll tell of His story, I'll tell of His love, and I'll tell of His goodness for me, how He purchased my redemption, with His own Blood, at from that, I have been set free. (Loose) Oh I am redeemed bought with a price, Jesus has changed my whole life, if anyone ask you, tell them I am redeemed. End song.

Apostle Peter was redeemed (Converted) on Pentecostal Day, and 120 more, plus 3,000 soul added, plus many more in the First Apostolic Church. There is many thousands, in these far off end time churches, that are being redeemed (converted), humble men and women, who obeys Acts 2:38-42. How does that song go, give me that old time religion, it was good enough for my father and it's good enough for me. Far off end time's day. Changes, who likes changes, not us, because we are all to set in our ways. God, says, today if you harden, not your hearts, and don't resist the Holy Ghost. You have the truth, now it's up to you this day, whom you serve. Jesus loves those who obey, get ready, get ready, He is coming. On those clouds don't wait till he closes those Pearly Gates. Saints, will come marching in, do you want yourself and family and friends and church members, march down those streets of glory. I know you care for your family, as much as Jesus loves us all. Tomorrow isn't promised to no one. Like a thief in the night, death comes, to us all, we can't stop that, but we can be ready for Eternal life, Oh how glad, that day shall be for saints, even us far off end time's men and women, true faith salvation. Don't stay in those chains, let Jesus lose them forevermore. Amen and Amen.

Chapter 2

John the Baptist was Elijah

Old Testament – OT

Malachi 4:5 Behold, I will send you Elijah the prophet before the coming of the great and dreadful day of the Lord.

New Testament – NT

Mark 1:1 The beginning of the gospel of Jesus Christ the Son of God; 2 As it is written in the prophets, Behold, I send my messenger before thy face, which shall prepare thy way before thee. 3 The voice of one crying in the wilderness, Prepare ye the way of the Lord, make his paths straight. 4 John did baptize in the wilderness and preach the baptism of repentance for the remission of sins. 8 I indeed have baptized you with water; but he shall baptize you the Holy Ghost. 9 And it came to pass in those days, that Jesus came from Nazareth of Galilee, and was baptized of John, thy water of Jordan.

John 3:22 After these things came Jesus and his disciples into the land of Judea; and there he tarried with them, and baptized. 23 And John also was baptizing in Aenon near to Salim, because there were much water there: and they came, and were baptized. 24 For John yet not cast into Prison. 25-36 Read these Scriptures. Verse 28 Ye yourselves bear me witness, that I said, I am not the Christ, but that I am sent before him.

Matthew 11:12 And from the days of John the Baptist until now the kingdom of Heaven suffereth violence, and the violent take it by force. 12 For all the prophets and the law prophesied until John. 14 And if ye will receive it, this is Elias, which was to come. Just think, Jesus' kingdom is here, to all who wants to enter into it. Started at Pentecostal First Apostolic preachers, plus 120, plus 3,000 souls. Right to these far off end times days, Acts 2:38-42 True Church. The world must enter into the Kingdom of God, only by, John 3:3-5 As we read the book of Acts, please read this, the Act of the Apostles, Apostle Paul wrote the Books, Acts, Romans, 1 Corinthians, 2 Corinthians, Galatians, Ephesians, Philippians, Colossians, 1 Thessalonians, 2 Thessalonians, 1 Timothy, 2 Timothy, Titus, Philemon, Hebrews, all books. So can we believe Apostle Paul's words of True Apostolic Church's start. Jesus opened Apostle Paul's blind eyes, Jesus want us all to come out of the darkness into the light, truth.

In Acts 9:1-16 15 But the Lord said unto him, go thy way, for the chosen vessel unto me, to bear my name before the Gentiles, and the children of Israel. 16 For I will show him how great that he must suffer for my names' sake. As we see how Jesus used Apostle Paul to bring the True Salvation to all, even us a far of men and women, to the very last Gentiles, Jesus' built church. If all those Apostles, preached the Acts 2:38-42 same way. As many Apostolic Churches Preach these days, who truly believes Bibles. Apostle Peter said in Acts 2:37-42. This is for everyone, even as many as our Lord god shall call. Then, how, even as time winds down for us all. John the Baptist prepared the way for Jesus to start the kingdom of God. Jesus wants to wash away all our sins in His lovely saving name. Acts 22:21 And he said unto me, Depart; for I will send thee far hence unto the (Gentiles.) Now as we see Jesus told Apostle Paul, to go and preach unto the (Gentiles.) You, then and now all a far off, end times. Oh how precious are those blessings given unto us, even 2,000 years later, in our lifetime, Apostle's true Doctrine, just like that Pentecostal Day. Acts 4:11 This is the stone (Jesus) which was set at nought of you builders, which is become the head of the corner. Verse 12 Neither is there salvation in any other, for there is none other name (Jesus) under heave given among men, whereby we must be saved. What name must we be baptized into the water, for the remission of sins. Acts 2:38 in Jesus Christ's name. Acts 19:5,6 5 when they heard this, they were baptized in the name of the Lord Jesus, 6 and when Paul laid his hands upon them, the Holy Ghost came on them, and they spake with tongues, and prophesied. John 14:17 Even the Spirit of Truth; whom the world cannot receive, because it seeth him not, neither knoweth him; but ye know him; for he dwelleth with you, and shall be in you. 18 I will not leave you comfortless; I will come to you. 2 Corinthians 13:5 Examine yourselves, whether ye be in the faith; prove your own selves. Know ye not your own selves, how that Jesus Christ is in you, except ye be reprobates? Galatians 3:27 For as many of you as have been baptized into Christ have put on Christ. Acts 2:37-42 Jesus Christ Acts 3:19, 20 Repent and ye therefore, and be converted, (to change beliefs) that your sins may be blotted out, when the times of refreshing shall come from the presence of the Lord; 20 And he shall send Jesus Christ, (Holy Ghost) which before was preached unto you.

Acts 11:13 And he shewed us how he had seen an angel in his home which stood and said unto him, send men to Joppa, and call for Simon, whose surname is Peter; 14 who shall tell these words, whereby thou and all thy house shall be saved. 15 And as I began to speak, the Holy Ghost fell on them, as on us at the beginning. 16 Then I remembered the word of the Lord, how that he said, John indeed baptized with water; but ye shall be baptized with the Holy Ghost. 17 Forasmuch then as God gave them the like gift as he did unto us, who believed on the Lord Jesus Christ; what was I, that I could withstand God? 18 When they heard these things, they held their peace pentance unto life. 19 Now they which were scattered abroad, upon the persecution that arose about Stephen travelled as far as Phenice, and Cyprus, and Antioch, preaching the word to none but unto the Jews, only. 26 And when he had found him, he brought (Paul) unto Antioch. And it came to pass, that a whole year they assembled themselves with the church, and taught much people. And the disciples were called Christians first in Antioch. From the Day of Pentecost in Acts 1:4 Acts 2:37-42 They preached Apostles true doctrine, baptized in (Jesus' loving name) for the remission of sins, and laying on hands to receive the gift of the Holy Ghost, spoke in tongues. Romans 1:16 For I am not ashamed of the Gospel of Christ: for it is the power of God unto salvation to everyone that believeth; to the Jew first, and also to the Greek. 1 Corinthians

2:10 but God has revealed them unto us by his Spirit; for the Spirit searcheth all things, yea the (deep) things of God. 3:7 So then neither is he that planeth anything, neither he that watereth; but God that giveth the increase. 18 Let no man deceive himself. If any man among you seemeth to be wise in this world, let him become a fool, that he may be wise.

Isaiah 28:9 Whom shall he teach knowledge? And whom shall he make to understand (doctrine)? Them that are weaned from the milk, and drawn from the breasts. 10 for precept must be upon precept, precept upon precept; line upon line, line upon line, here a little and there a little. 11 for with stammering lips and another (tongue) will he speak to this people. 12 to whom he said, this is the rest where with ye may cause the weary to rest; and this is the refreshing: (yet) they would not hear. 13 But the word of the Lord was unto them precept upon precept, precept upon precept; line upon line, line upon line; here a little, and there a little; that they might go, and fall backward and be broken and snared, and taken. Romans 10: How then shall they call on him in whom they have not believed? And how shall they believe in him of whom they have not heard? And how shall they hear without a preacher?

Chapter 2: Mark (T) for true and (F) for False

1. – T-or-F- In Malachi 4:5 Behold, I will send you Elijah the prophet before the coming of the great and dreadful day of the Lord.

2. – T-or-F- In Matthew 3:3 For this is he that was spoken of by the prophet Esaias, saying, the voice of one crying in the wilderness, prepare ye the way of the Lord, make the paths straight.

3. – T-or-F- In Matthew 3:11 I indeed baptize with water unto repentance: but he that cometh after me is mightier than I, whose shoes I am not worthy to bear: he shall baptize you with the Holy Ghost, and with fire.

4. – T-or-F- Matthew 11:12-14 And from the days of John the Baptist until now the kingdom of heaven suffereth violence, and the violent take it by force. 13 For all the prophets and the law prophesied until John 14 And if ye will receive it, this is Elias, which was for to come.

5. – T-or-F- Mark 1:3 The voice of one crying in the wilderness, prepare ye the way of the Lord, make his paths straight.

6. – T-or-F- Luke 3:4 As it is written in the book of the words of Esaias the prophet, saying, the voice of one crying in the wilderness. Prepare ye the way of the Lord, make his path straight.

7. – T-or-F- Luke 7:27 This is he, of whom it is written, behold I send my messenger before thy face, which shall prepare thy way before thee.

8. – T-or-F- John 1:23 He said, I am the voice of one crying in the wilderness, make straight the way of the Lord, as sayeth the prophet Esaias

9. – T-or-F- John 3:28 Ye yourselves bear me witness, that I said, I am not the Christ, but that I am sent before him.

10. – T-or-F- John 5:33 Ye sent unto John, and he bare witnesseth unto the truth. 35 He was a burning and a shining light, and ye were willing for a season to rejoice in his light.

Chapter 3

Horseshoe Games

This is one of the oldest games in America, just a time to enjoy moments and memories with family and friends, mostly on picnic days. Oh I truly miss those 4th of July Days, each perfect summer moments. It wasn't about wins or lost, it was only about spending time together. The horseshoe game was to 21 points, first there won the fun game. A stake was placed down in the ground, two pits, square wooden pits, each pit was set same amount apart, with metal stakes in center of each pit. One or two players at each pit, four horseshoes to each pit, gold or silver or number one or number two horseshoes, first player throws one show, then second shoe, the third horseshoe, then at the other pit, they measured the distance of all four horseshoes, first they check for ringers, then they check for leaners up against the pole stakes, then they check for closeness to the pole. Now if the shoe is outside the distance of a horseshoe there isn't no point, if the horseshoe is in a horseshoe measure, it counts as one point, then a leaner counts as two points, but a ringer counts as 3 points. Then the next pit player throws the other three, they check for points again. When a player hits twenty one, the game is finish, then onto next game. Only one place, no second place in this fun game, just first place wins. Now we know the rules, a win (victor) finish the race, game, or contest. I'm trying to help everyone understand, first place only is true wins. Just like a horseshoe, that isn't close to the metal stake, no chance.

A nonbeliever, no faith in God, outside of Salvation, no care, one way or other. Unless God increases his faith, or remain atheistic, infidel as unbelievers. Next a horseshoe close to metal stake, closer one gets appoint. Someone that has faith in God, is a leaner type, trusts in God. Then there comes Ringer, someone that obeys god's true salvation. In Acts 2:38-42 Repent, then be baptized in (Jesus') lovely name. And believes God's gift of the Holy Ghost filling, by speaking in tongues. As all the Acts – Books – as the true Apostle's brothers and sisters did Pentecostal Day 120 and 3,000 more obeyed the Apostolic True Church. Then work out your own Salvation with fear and trembling. Philippians 2:12 1 Timothy 2:15 Study, Study, Study, the word of truth. Apostle Paul, finish the race, because he obeyed the Acts 2:38-42 Gospel truth. I pray we all finish this race, there isn't no second place or third place. Salvation isn't a game, your Eternal life depends upon true Apostles words.

Horse Shoes and Baseball Games

The all-time American Baseball game, from start to finish, first place. Get your hot dogs and cokes, these words of moments in our lifetimes. Your team is counting on your support as great fans, cheer them on batter up, is being called, players are all ready for action to begin, any moment. The pitcher throws the fast curve ball, the batter swings and missed, strike one, pitcher throws the second fast ball, batter misses again, the pitcher has the batter nervous now, so he throws the third ball hard and fast. Sadly the batter strikes out, one, two, three, you're out, umpire calls out. One and on, goes the game, till the game is finished, or postponed, to a next day. Horseshoes, baseball games, are fun and exciting, family's join to cheer on. When life is started, as a child, we start going to Sunday School classes, then teenage Bible Studies, next step in the Big Church groups, then study to be a Preacher, Bishop, or a Priest, maybe a Pope or Minister. The harder we study for truth, higher figure (Apostolic) spot. Acts 2:38-42 And they continued steadfastly in the (Apostle's doctrine) and fellowship, and in the breaking of bread, and in prayers. Hebrews 6:1 1 Therefore leaving the principles of the (doctrine of Christ) let us go on unto perfection; not laying (again) the foundation of repentance from (dead works) and of faith toward God, 2 of the doctrine of baptisms, and laying on of hands, and of resurrection of the dead, and of eternal judgment. 1 Peter 3:21 the Like figure where unto ever baptism doth also (now saves us) not the putting away of the filth of the flesh, but the answer of a good conscience toward God, by the resurrection of Jesus Christ. John 3:3-8 Water and spirit.

Olympic Games, started in Ancient Greek, then in 1896, modern Internatio0nal sport every four years, everyone works hard for those Gold, silver and bronze medals. Years of training and practice, you don't want second place silver or third place bronze. The gold medal holders brag and talk, all their life, they earned that title, right. This world's glory in life, they cherish (hold dear) treasure this prize gold medal. It is spoken about for generations in families, their heroes, just like Samson. The Golden gloves, boxing glove's hall of famous fighters of all-time greats. These medals, men and women, all the people in all the ages, earned those Gold prize. Some broke records, new titles, something to be proud of for life time. Now gold is very important metal, like rings, crowns, church plates, candle holders, gold watch or band, bracelet, cross, every important thing, your cherish in life.

True or False – Chapter -3- T-or-F- Questions

1.) – T-or-F- In Genesis 2:16, 17 Did Adam get a command from God not to eat from tree of knowledge, that if he ate of it, he would die?

2.) – T-or-F- In Genesis 5:5 – Did Adam die at the Age of 930 years?

3.) – T-or-F- In Genesis 9:11-17 was it a covenant between God and man, that He would not destroy the Earth again, form the floods?

4.) – T-or-F- In Genesis 11:1 was there only one language on Earth?

5.) – T-or-F- In Genesis 11:7-9 Did the Lord confound their language and scatter them all over the Earth from the tower of Babel?

6.) – T-or-F- In Genesis 40:1-23 Did God use Joseph in prison, to save the land of Egypt and his own family and nation?

7.) – T-or-F- In 2 Kings was Naaman cured after he washed in the river, seven times, from leper?

8.) – T-or-F- In Matthew 3:1-11 Was John the Baptist baptizing everyone in the river, even the Pharisees and Sadducees, for repentance?

9.) – T-or-F- In Acts 1:12-16 Did the 120 get the gift of the Holy Ghost as they all spoke in tongues? 2:1-4 verse 3, tongues of fire?

10.) – T-or-F- in Acts 2:37, Did they ask Peter and the rest of the Apostles what shall we do?

11.) – T-or-F- Did Peter say to them the sinners prayer, just believe and trust in Jesus, and you are saved? In Acts 2:38

12.) – T-or-F- Did Peter say just repent? In Acts 2:38

13.) – T-or-F- In the Acts 2:38 page, did Peter say get baptized in the name of (Jesus Christ) for the remission of sins?

14.) – T-or-F- In Acts 8:15-18 verse 12 Then Simon himself believed also, and when he was baptized in Jesus' name, was he saved there?

15.) – T-or-F- In Acts 8:17-19 Did Simon the Sorcery receive the gift, as hands was laid on others, since he also believed and was baptized in Jesus name?

16.) – T-or-F- In Acts 10:42-48 Did Peter again command those also that just receive the Holy Ghost gift as they spoke in tongues, as well as we to be baptized in Jesus'?

17.) – T-or-F- In Acts 18:24, 25 Did they only know the baptism of John's in repentance?

18.) – T-or-F- In Acts 19:1-7 Did Apostle Paul rebaptize them again in Jesus' name, and then laid his hands on them, till they spake with tongues, as all twelve, received the gift of the Holy Ghost?

Chapter 4

God's Hidden Treasures, Gold, Silver, Polished

Old Testament – OT

Genesis 37:28 Then there passed by Midianites merchantmen; and they drew and lifted up Joseph out of the pit, and sold Joseph to the Ishmaelites for twenty pieces of silver, and they brought Joseph into Egypt. 36 And the Midianites sold him into Egypt unto Potiphar, and officer of Pharaoh's, and captain of the guard. 39:2 And the Lord was with Joseph, and he was a prosperous man, and he was in the house of his master the Egyptian. 3 And his master saw that the Lord was with him, and the Lord made all that he did to prosper in his hands. Joseph was shaped and mold, to be used by God, in that Prison, to feed all the lands of Egypt, and all the nations.

Exodus 2:10 And the child grew, and she brought him unto Pharaoh's daughter, and he became her son. And she called his name Moses: and she said, 'Because I drew him out of the water.' As we see God's hands shaping and mold, Moses into shape, to be used as a (deliver) set free, God's chosen people, children of Israel. Now as we read how God prepared and shaped Moses, Moses said who am I to do this? Moses' question was honest, because God, knew Moses' past, his anger in life, quick temper. God's ways isn't like man's way, God knows man's true heart. Not where he was, or is now in life, God know his work, just how to mold, shape and polish, into a right heart, mind and spirit. David, as a king of Israel, in Psalm 51:1-12 1- Create in me a clean heart, O God; and renew a right spirit within me. As the Bible says, God knows the future or man's heart. We can only see the past or present day, no one has a chance to be saved, till God starts shaping and mold, then polish his mind and heart no one is ready for God's use, until God's work is started in action. Jonah the biggest fish story ever read, as an example to us all. 1:1-17 Jonah hated those people in Nineveh that great city of wickedness. So Jonah sailed the other way, but, God, brought him to Nineveh by a big fish, then Jonah preached, what he was first told to do. God had washed and polish Jonah, to a new way of thinking, right.

America, is known as the leader of the World in all things. Sadly, years ago they changed this U.S. America into a sad country. A governor decided to change the law, to life means life, no chance, no one earns days off, for good credit, GED, Programs, NA, AAA, or other self-help programs, specific projects groups, rehabilitation change of life. I have watched Lifers leave this prison, after giving time back, thank to other great men here, helped make a way out for them, Praise god. Those men became preachers, halfway houses projects, leaders to those younger generations, they know how to set them straight in life's walks.

The world needs these Gold and silver, polished, shaped and molded men and women, fathers, mothers, aunts, uncles, big brothers and sister, family. Like a great President, once told, tear down those walls, let the people go, he told the other country, nation, they tore down those walls. God says tear down those prison walls for my Gold and silver prison men and women, let my shaped and molded and polish, go home. Let them lead others, this generation, to next generations to come. You took the Bible out of schools, courthouses, you need these men and women to teach their families, how to walk the right paths.

I believe Norway is the Country, that helps their men and women change generations, by an example, 6 months for all crimes, if you are a mass murder, you spend 12 years in prison, when you are punished, (penalty) for crime, you spend time in your own house, they built for crime breakers, you go to your job, they truly rehabilitate you. This great USA, could really learn something about those Great prison walls, coming down, it is time to walk the talk, not just talk. Reform in USA, is a slow progress, future, always in the future. Let America become a great nation again, why put off till tomorrow, what you can do today, this day, this day, tear down walls. Some mean and women, has twenty, thirty, forty, fifty years already in. They are already leaders, behind these great prison walls, yes great leaders. Some have lead men and women towards straight paths in life. I truly thank God, for these great men, in this prison, men who helped me get my life, straighten out right, men who prayed for me, with me, and year around.

I thank God, three times a day, for dying for all my sins in life. Praise the Lord, He gives us time to turn our lives around, second, third, fourth, fifth, He shapes and mold and polish us, each one by one, into His image, to be fit for the kingdom of

God. The judge says, you don't deserve a second chance, how sad those words. God doesn't look for a perfect man or woman, He says, come to me, as you are, I will not forsake or turn you away, I'll be your Father, Brother, your friend, My kingdom is just for born again. All can enter not just those perfect saints, but, by my Grace and Mercy. Who shall tear those walls down? Norway, isn't just words, it's truly a reform built country, home of the free and proud, people I'll always think and know about these great men and women, behind these prison walls, I can't wait till God, sets them free. Gold and silver, polished, fit to come out, from these great walls. Jesus, isn't just a name, it's a name above all names on Earth, and in heaven, build his kingdom, don't bury or hid his Gold and silver polished treasures, Men and women, who can change this USA.

Yes, we could write Scriptures, but, sometimes it's best to write things. Scriptures are past tense, today or tomorrow is very important to us also. The Bible says in, Matthew 25:43 I was a stranger, and ye took me not in naked, and ye clothed me not; sick, and in prison, and ye visited me not. 25:44 Then shall they also answer him, saying Lord, when saw we thee, a hungered, or thirst, and did not minister unto thee? 45 then shall he answer them, saying, verily I say unto you, in as much as yet did it not to one of the least of these, ye did it not to me. Oh how sad, those words. Well, I could have helped those men or women, but, I put it off to another (governor) or (president) not today, maybe tomorrow, next term, they can wait, but, these great men and women, can and will change the USA, generations, and generations to come, leaders, knowing the walk. It is not what the country, can do for you, it is what you can do for your country, today, not to another (Governor or President) to end.

Chapter -4- Questions – True (T) – False (F)

1.) –T- or –F- Revelation 21:10-27 Are you in the Lamb's book of life.

2.) –T-or-F- 1 Peter 3:21 Doth baptism now save us?

3.) – T-or –F- Acts 4:10-12 – What name was there for salvation, Jesus?

4.) – T –or- F- Matthew 7:21-23 Did they cast out devils in Jesus' name?

5.) – T –or- F- Matthew 15:9 Are you in the doctrines of men?

6.) – T –or- F- Are you following the Doctrine of Apostle Peter? Acts 2:38

7.) –T –or- F- Acts 19:1-6 Have you spake with tongues since you believed?

8.) – T –or- F- Mark 1:24 Did the evil spirit ask Jesus not to destroy him?

9.) – T –or- F- Mark 12:29 Did Jesus says the Lord our God is one Lord?

10.) –T –or- F- Mark 16:15-17 Did Jesus say, he that believeth and is baptized shall be saved; and he that believeth not shall be damned?

11.) –T- or- F- Mark 16:17 Did Jesus say in his name, they shall cast out devils' they shall speak new tongues?

12.) –T- or- F- Luke 2:11 was Jesus born a Saviour?

13.) –T- or- F- Isaiah 43:3, 10-15 Did God say he was the only Saviour?

14.) –T- or- F- Isaiah 9:6 Is Jesus the Mighty God, the Everlasting Father?

15.) –T- or- F- Daniel 7:9, 10 Is there only One throne set for the Ancient of Days, Judgment when books opened?

16.) –T- or- F- Zechariah 14:1, 5-9 Is Jesus coming with his saints, and in that shall there be only one Lord and his name one?

17.) –T- or- F- Revelation 1:12-18 Is Jesus the Ancient of days, is he also the first and the last, and was dead, and has the key of hell.

18.) – T- or –F- Revelation 4:1-11 was twenty elders worshiping the one throne with God on it?

19.) –T- or- F- Revelation 11:16 Did twenty elders sat before God's throne and fall on their faces to worship him?

20.) –T- or- F- Revelation 19:1-16 Is Jesus King of Kings and Lord of Lords?

21.) –T- or- F- Revelation 21:5 How many thrones, are there only one?

Chapter 5

Moses' Books to John's Revelation Book

From Genesis to Revelation, God's limit time for ma. Moses explains in Genesis 1:1-16 and God made two great light the greater light to rule the day, and the lesser light to rule the night; he made the stars also. For season, and for days and years. Time. Everyone knows time, to be born, and a time to die, set for us all. Moses, was taught by Pharaoh's wise men. Astrology he mastered faster. God had Moses life prepared, from birth, to be the (deliverer). As we all read and know the walk out of Egypt, for the Israelites. Next, the Exodus Book tells in 20:1-26 11 for in six days the Lord made heaven and earth, the sea, and all that in them is, and rested the seventh day: wherefore the Lord blessed the Sabbath day, and hallowed it. 7th day. Exodus 20:1-36 How the Ten commandments, God wrote on stones. God wants everyone to love and worship him, from Adam and Eve, to last born. In the Old Testament, Moses told how God walked and talked with Adam and Eve in the garden. Genesis 3:8 Read the verse Noah was saved by the Ark, tree built, sins was washed away by water. Tree and water, in the NT New Testament. 1 Peter 3:20 which sometimes were disobedient, when once the long suffering of God waited in the days of Noah, while the (ark) was preparing, where in few, that is eight souls were saved by water. 21 The like figure whereunto even baptism doth also (now) save us (not the putting away of the filth of the flesh) but the answer of a good conscience toward God, by the resurrection of Jesus Christ. Can you see how the Old Testament (intertwines) with NW. Genesis 11:1 the whole earth was of one language, and of one speech. 11:5 And the Lord came down to see the city and the tower, which the men built. 11:9 Therefore is the name of it called Babel; because the Lord did there confound the language of all the earth; and from thence did the Lord scatter them abroad upon the face of all the earth. Daniel 12:4 But thou, O Daniel, shut up the words, and seal the book, even to the time of the end; many shall run to and fro, and knowledge shall be increased. Matthew 24:14 And this Gospel of the kingdom shall be preached in all the world for a witness unto (all) nations; and then shall the end come.

In, Joel 2:27-29 God said "I will pour out my (spirit) upon all flesh." As we read in Acts 1, 2:38-42 God started pouring out his (spirit). It has been about 2,000 years, how long do we have left, before, Jesus comes for his saints, the rapture shall soon take place, if you are not born again, as Jesus said in John 3:3-5. And as Peter said in Acts 2:38-42 Baptized in Jesus' lovely name for the (remission of your sins) then as you receive the (gift) Holy Ghost filled by speaking in tongues. Sadly, you shall not be in the rapture, the great (7 year) tribulation, shall you be stuck in, as you see now the (3rd war) has already starting to line up. Every nation is picking sides, how many signs must you see.

The world has enough nuclear power missile (rockets) to blow world up now. If you read in 1 Kings 18:13-40 There was 450 false prophets, back in there time, now just think about how many millions there are in this time and age. In Matthew 15:9 teaching doctrines of men. In Matthew 16:18, 19 Jesus said unto Peter, I will give unto you the keys of the kingdom of heaven. In Acts 2:38-42 Apostle Peter started binding on (Earth and Heaven) the name of men and women, who obeyed the words in Acts 2:38-42 what name (Jesus' name) baptism, and God gave the (gift) of the Holy Ghost (Spirit, as that 120 spoke in tongues, plus 3,000 souls were added (binded on Earth and Heaven.) Acts 2:38-42 Peter said this is for you, your children and even for (all) who are a far off, as many as the Lord our God shall call. Who are you following, Apostles, which Doctrine are you in, false doctrine, or Acts 2:38-42. In Romans 1:16, 25 Who changed the truth? 8:1-11 Spirit? Romans 14:18 Apostle Paul spoke tongues and he laid hands of others till they spoke in tongues. Acts 11:1-21 the gift was still given to them. In Acts 19:1-6 The same doctrine, as in the beginning. Like Apostle Peter spoke in Acts 2:38-42 This is for you, your children, even to those who are (a far off) last days in time, yes for us all. Revelation 20:6 No power, on such, the second death as on 20:5-15 Brothers and sisters, follow Apostle's doctrine in Acts 2:38-42 Don't be outside the Holy City, when the fire comes from God.

The Gospel is being preached, to all Nations, radio, T.V., phones, books, iPod, so much knowledge and easy ways to gather the Gospel, so as we all know now, the End Time is coming close to, Jesus' second coming, riding clouds just like

He did in Old Testament O.T. Psalm 104:3 Who layeth the beams of his chambers in the water; who maketh the clouds his chariot, who walketh upon the wings of the wind. Acts 1:9 And when he had spoken these things, while they beheld, he was taken up; and a cloud perceived him out of their sight. Daniel 7:9 I behold till the thrones were cast down, and the (Ancient of days) did set, whose garment was white as snow and the hair of his head like pure wool; his throne was like the fiery flame, and his wheels as burning fire. 10 A fiery stream issued and came forth form before him, and thousand thousands ministered unto him, and ten thousand times ten thousand stood before him, the judgement was set, and the books were opened. 13 I saw in the night visions, and behold, one like the son of man came with the clouds of heaven, and came to the Ancient of days, and they brought him near before him. 14 And there was given him dominions, and glory, and a kingdom, that all people, nations, and languages, should serve him; his dominion is an everlasting domino, which shall pass not away, that which shall not be destroyed.

Now brothers and sisters, are you really truly born again, of water and spirit. Saint Peter spoke the Jesus' built Apostolic Doctrine True Gospel. Not those watered down man made, just believe and you're saved, by faith. Your Eternal life, you best search the search those scripture. John 5:39, 40 Who, will stand at your side on judgement day, not those preachers, who watered down, Acts 2:38-42 Saint Peter's words to us all, to the end. God is not, taking away from those preachers, He is trying to reach out to them, so they can preach the Acts 2:38-42. True salvation. Moses to Revelation, Books of life, start to end of time, soon finishing. Twinkle of an eye, we can be taken away, or left behind. Oh how close to Jesus' second coming, we all are now, please brothers and sister. Search like your Eternal life depends upon it, because it really truly does. Those days of Early first church is still open, for us all, these end time days are here, who knows the hour, but, God is trying to get you out of darkness, into Jesus' light, wake up world, don't sleep, awake out of the darkness, search, search like never before, time is winding out.

In Joel 2:27-29 God said "I will pour out my (Spirit) upon all flesh." As we read in Acts 1, 2:38-42 God started pouring out his (Spirit). It has been about 2,000 years, how long do we have left, before Jesus comes for his saints, the Rapture shall soon take place, if you are not born again, as Jesus said in John 3:3-5 And as Peter said in Acts 2:38-42 Baptized in Jesus' lovely name for the (remission of your sins). Then as your receive the (gift) Holy Ghost filled by speaking in tongues. Sadly, you shall not be in the Rapture, the great (7 year) Tribulation, shall you be stuck in, as you see now the (3rd War) has already starting, to line up every nation is picking sides, how many signs, must you see.

The world has enough nuclear power missile (rockets) to blow world up now. If you read in 1 Kings 18:13-40 There was 450 False Prophets back in their time, now just think about how many millions there are in this time and age. In Matthew 15:9 teaching doctrines of men. In Matthew 16:18, 19 Jesus said unto Peter, I will give unto you the keys of the kingdom of heaven. In Acts 2:38-42 Apostle Peter started binding on (Earth and Heaven) the names of men and women, who obeyed the words in, Acts 2:38-42 what name (Jesus' name) baptism, and God gave the (gift) of the Holy Ghost (Spirit), as that 120 spoke in tongues, plus 3,000 souls were added (binded on Earth and Heaven). Acts 2:38-42 Peter said, this is for you, your children and even, for (all) who are a far off, as many as the Lord our God shall call. Who are you following, Apostles which Doctrine are you in, false Doctrine, or Acts 2:38-42. In Romans 1:16, 25 Who changed the truth? 8:1-11 Spirit? Romans 14:18 Apostle Paul spoke tongues and he laid hands of others till they spoke in tongues. Acts 11:1-21 the gift was still given to them. In Acts 19:1-6 The same doctrine as in the beginning. Like Apostle Peter spoke in Acts 2:38-42 This is for you, your children, even to those who are (a far off) last days in time, yes for us all. Revelation 20:6 No Power on such, the second death has on. 20:5-15 Brothers and sisters, follow Apostle's doctrine in Acts 2:38-42 Don't be outside the Holy City when the fire comes from God.

True (T) or False (F) Questions

1.) – T-or-F- In Deuteronomy 32:39, Did God say? Verse 39 See now that I, even I, am he, and there is no god with me: I kill, and I make alive; I wound, and I heal; neither is there any that can deliver out of my hand.

2.) – T-or-F- In Nehemiah 9:6 Did thou say, art Lord Alone?

3.) – T-or-F- In Job 9:8 Did he alone spreadeth out the heavens, and walks upon the sea?

4.) – T-or-F- In Psalm 68: 4 Was God said to rideth the Heavens, and his name, JAH?

5.) – T-or-F- Was the name Jehovah alone? Psalm 83:18

6.) – T-or-F- In Psalm 86:10 did it say thou art God alone?

7.) – T-or-F- In Psalm 104:3 Did God make clouds his chariot?

8.) – T-or-F- In Psalm 124:8 Is our help in the name of the Lord?

9.) – T-or-F- In Isaiah 7:14 was a son to be born, and called Immanuel?

10.) – T-or-F- In Isaiah 9:6 was that son, to be called, the Mighty God, and Everlasting Father?

11.) – T-or-F- In Isaiah 42:1-8 Did God say He wouldn't share glory?

12.) – T-or-F- In Isaiah 43:3, 10-18 Did God say, he was the only Saviour?

13.) – T-or-F- In Isaiah 44:6, 8, 24 Did God say, I am the first and I am the last; and beside me there is no god? Verse 24 Lord Alone.

14.) – T-or-F- In Isaiah 45: 6, 11, 12, 15, 18, 21, 23 Did God say he done all his self?

15.) – T-or-F- In Zechariah 14:5-9 Is God coming with all the saints and in that day, was in to be only one Lord and his name one?

16.) – T-or-F- In Malachi 4:5 Did it say the Lord was coming on that great and dreadful day, after Elijah came?

17.) – T-or-F- In Mark 2:10 Did Jesus have power to forgive sins?

18.) – T-or-F- In Matthew 28:18 Did Jesus say All power is given unto me in heaven and in earth?

19.) – T-or-F- In John 10:18-30 Did Jesus say that I and my Father are one?

20.) – T-or-F- In John 14:6-18 Did Jesus say that he was also the Father and the Holy Ghost?

Chapter 6

God's First Blood Sacrifice to God's Last Sacrifice

As we start this Chapter in this book we shall start in Genesis 2:17. 17- But of the tree of knowledge of (good and evil), thou shalt not eat of it. 3:6 And when the woman saw that the tree was good for food, and that it was pleasant to the eyes, and a tree to be desired to make one wise, she took of the fruit thereof, and did eat, and gave also unto her husband with her; and he did eat. 3:21 Unto Adam also and to his wife did the Lord God make coats of skins, and clothes them. First Blood. Now we go to Noah, after the (Great flood). Genesis 8:20-22. 20 and Noah built an altar unto the Lord; and took of every clean beast, and of every clean fowl, and offered burnt offering on the alter. 21 and the Lord smelled a sweet savour; and the Lord said in his heart, I will not again curse the ground any more for man's sake; for the imagination of man's heart is evil form his youth: neither will I again smite anymore everything living, as I have done. 22 While the earth remaineth, seed time and harvest and cool and heat and summer and winter, and day and night shall not cease. 9:13 I do set my bow in the clouds, and it shall be for a token of a covenant between me and the earth. God shows us His promise in, Ezekiel 1:26 And above the firmament that was over their heads was the likeness of a throne, as the appearance of a sapphire stone: and upon the likeness of the throne was the likeness as the appearance of a man above upon it. 27 And I saw a the colour of amber, as the appearance of fire around about with in it, from the appearance of his loins even upward, and from the appearance of his loins even downward, I saw as it were the appearance of fire, and it had brightness round about. 28 As the appearance of the bow that is in the cloud in the day of rain, so was the appearance of the brightness round about. This was the appearance of the likeness of the glory of the Lord. And when I saw it, I fell upon my face, when I heard a voice of one that spake. Revelation 4:1-11 After this I looked, and, behold, a door was opened in heaven; and the first voice which I heard was it as of a trumpet talking with me, which said, come up hither, and I will shew thee things which must be hereafter. 2 And immediately I was in the Spirit; and, behold, a throne was set in heaven, and one sat on the throne.

Song Chapter -6-

This is my story, this is my song praising my savior, all the day long

Born in his spirit, washed in his blood, praising my savior all the day long.

This is my story, this is my song, praising my savior, all the day long

End

Oh how blessed we all are to be chose by God. That He died for all our sins, from Adam and Eve, to us, even to the last day, in time. Someday soon, time shall be no more, heaven with our Lord. The New Heavens and Earth, Holy City coming down from Heaven. Streets of Pure Gold, Throne of God, pure river of water. No more night, neither light of the sun, Oh what a day that shall be.

Revelation 21:1 and I saw a new heaven and a new earth, for the first heaven and the first earth were passed away; and there was no more sea. 21:2 And I John saw the Holy City, New Jerusalem, coming down from God out of heaven, prepared as a bride adorned for her husband.

As we slowly read these Chapters 21, 22 I hope and pray these words, wakes everyone from darkness towards the light. Tick, Tock, Jesus is calling, don't be hard of hearing, don't be like King Agrippa. Acts 26:28 Then Agrippa said unto Paul, almost thou persuades me to be a Christian. Oh how sad, so close, almost. Men and women, don't be left behind, God has prepared all things. New Heaven, New Earth, New Holy City forever more, come to light. Choice is yours, Acts 2:38-42 True

Doctrine. Not watered down, is for us all, even to these end far off days in time. Amen. Amen.

Revelation 4:3 And he that sat was to look upon like a jasper and a sardine stone, and there was a rainbow round about the throne, in sight like unto an emerald. When God makes a covenant of the rainbow, He keeps His promise. In Genesis 15:18 In that same day the Lord made a covenant with Abram, saying unto thy seed have I giving this land, from the river of Egypt unto the great river, the river of Euphrates. In Isaiah 42:5-9 verse 6 I the Lord have called thee in righteousness, and will hold thine hand, and will keep thee and give thee for a covenant of the people, for alight of the Gentiles; 43: 3, 10-15 Exodus 12:17-23 God passed over, when the blood was on the doors. Leviticus 17:11 For the life of the flesh is in the blood; and I have given it to you upon the alter to make an atonement for your souls; for it is the blood that maketh an atonement for the soul.

In Matthew 20:28 Even as the Son of Man came not to be ministered unto but to minister and to give his life a ransom for many. Read John 19:10-30 Jesus said it is finished and he died. John 20:1-31 Jesus rose from the grave, after 3 days. In 2 Corinthians 5:10 For we must all appear before the judgement according to that he hath done, whether it be good or bad. Read Hebrews 2:9 But we see Jesus who was made a little lower than the angels for the suffering of (death) crowned with glory and honor; that he by the grace of God should taste death for every men. Acts 4:7-12 Neither is there salvation in any other; for there is none other name under heaven given among men, whereby we must be saved. Acts 19:1-6 verse 5 when they heard this, they were baptized in the name of the Lord Jesus.

JESUS' APOSTLES - TRUE BORN AGAIN DOCTRINE

Questions – True (T) or False (F)

1.) – T-or-F- In Genesis 3:21 Did God make coats of skins and clothes Adam and Eve?

2.) – T-or-F- In Genesis 4:1-7 Was Cain offering accepted by God?

3.) – T-or-F- In Genesis 15:1-21 Did God accept Abram's offering?

4.) – T-or-F- In Exodus 12:16-28 Had God made a sacrifice for Israel?

5.) – T-or-F- In 1 Samuel 15:22-23 Did Samuel say to obey the Lord is better than sacrifices?

6.) – T-or-F- In 1 Kings 18:13-40 was false prophets, way more than true prophets in those days?

7.) – T-or-F- In Psalm 51:1-17 Did God accept a broken spirit and a contrite heart?

8.) – T-or-F- In Exodus 10:1 Was Pharaoh's heart hardened by God?

9.) – T-or-F- In Isaiah 53:1-6 Was God going to lay all our iniquities on him?

10.) – T-or-F- In Matthew 7:21-23 Did Jesus say, they would cast out devils in his name, and do many wonderful works, but he profess, I never knew you?

11.) – T-or-F- In Matthew 16:15-19 Was Peter giving the keys to the kingdom of heaven, to bind or loose on earth and heaven?

12.) – T-or-F- In Matthew 18:3 Did Jesus say, except ye be converted?

13.) – T-or-F- In Matthew 20:28 Was Jesus to give his life for many?

14.) – T-or-F- In Matthew 24:11 Did Jesus say there was going to be many false prophets and shall deceive many?

15.) – T-or-F- In Acts 1:1-14 were they commanded to wait in Jerusalem until, they received the power of the Holy Ghost?

16.) – T-or-F- In Acts 2:1-4 Was Holy Ghost sitting on them as they spoke in tongues?

17.) – T-or-F- In Acts 2:37 Did they ask Peter, what they shall do?

18.) – T-or-F- In acts 2:38-42 Did Peter say, repent and get baptized in Jesus' name for the remission of sins and ye shall receive the gift of the Holy Ghost, for you and your children and all who are a far off?

Chapter 7

Fool's Gold

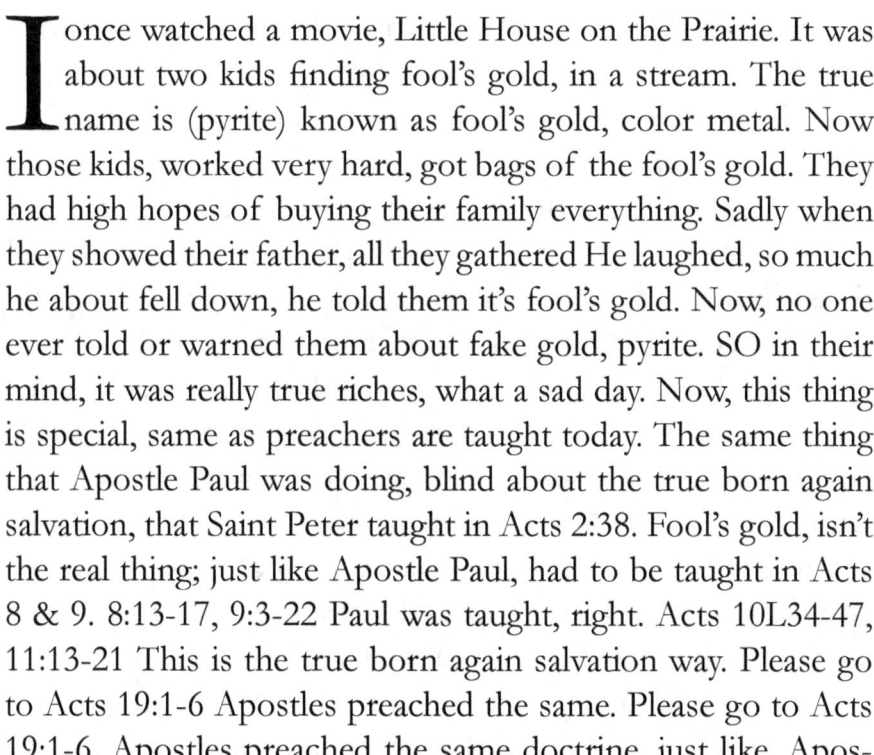

I once watched a movie, Little House on the Prairie. It was about two kids finding fool's gold, in a stream. The true name is (pyrite) known as fool's gold, color metal. Now those kids, worked very hard, got bags of the fool's gold. They had high hopes of buying their family everything. Sadly when they showed their father, all they gathered He laughed, so much he about fell down, he told them it's fool's gold. Now, no one ever told or warned them about fake gold, pyrite. SO in their mind, it was really true riches, what a sad day. Now, this thing is special, same as preachers are taught today. The same thing that Apostle Paul was doing, blind about the true born again salvation, that Saint Peter taught in Acts 2:38. Fool's gold, isn't the real thing; just like Apostle Paul, had to be taught in Acts 8 & 9. 8:13-17, 9:3-22 Paul was taught, right. Acts 10L34-47, 11:13-21 This is the true born again salvation way. Please go to Acts 19:1-6 Apostles preached the same. Please go to Acts 19:1-6, Apostles preached the same doctrine, just like, Apostolic Churches do this end time days. False preachers preach (pyrite), fool's gold, not real true salvation. Oh, it sounds good to the ears and mind and hearts, but, oh how sad, to think you're saved but sadly, still lost in your sins. Jesus' name, preached in the early First Church, till the Romans changed from Jesus' name to Trinity, as Father, Son and Holy Ghost. Paul warned about those wolfs, coming in the church, changing the true gospel born again salvation, into (pyrite) fake gold. These preachers found (pyrite) not the real truth, real gold words. Just believe, that isn't what those Apostles preached, they gave their lives, for us all, first church end time last days of life. Make it easy, just believe. Acts 19:1-6 Paul rebaptized them into Jesus' lovely name, then laid hands on them, till they spake with tongues. Same in Acts 2:38-42 For everyone, not just that day, but, to the last man, end time days, Apostolic churches, still preach these days.

Today you can find anything you want in about 5-10 minutes. How easy to search things, your Eternal Life, depends on your own time, you listen to a movie or a play or T.V. show, hours at a time. As the Corinthians 2:9, 10 for the Spirit searcheth all things. Now a preachers might tell you, you're saved by faith. That preacher isn't going to be standing with you at the throne. If you read Acts 2:38-42 Saint Peter, tells the truth. All eternal life, depends on your search for the true salvation. Apostle Paul warned, about false preachers sounding really good. He wrote most of the New Testaments, he said brothers, so that was to brothers already in the true faith, ones all was saved. If Apostle Peter and Paul rebaptized them into Jesus' name, then why not follow those true salvation, Apostle's same ways.

When the Bible says, there is no other name, where to be saved. John 3:3-10 Born of the (water and Spirit) Jesus' words, spoken. Apostles in Acts started the true born again of water and Spirit. There is many Apostolic Churches in every town and city, today. Do you want fool's gold or gold streets, you must search. All saints, will follow Jesus, are you a sheep of Christ Jesus? Is your eyes open to the true saving salvation, Acts 2:38-42? Or will you follow the lost preacher, that was blinded by the devil. Acts 19:1-6 please read this till your eyes open and follow Saint Peter and Paul's true salvation. Acts 2:37-42 37 Now when they heard this, they were pricked in the heart, and said unto Peter and the rest of the Apostles, men and brethren, what shall we do? 38 Then Peter said unto them, repent, and be baptized every one of you in the name of Jesus Christ for the (remission of sins), and ye shall receive the gift of the Holy Ghost. 39 For the promise is for you and your children, and to (all) that are (a far off) even as many as the Lord our God, shall call. Now even today, these Apostolic Churches preach the very same Acts 2:42 Apostle's Doctrine.

Chapter -7- Fool's Gold —Questions T or F

1.) – T-or-F- In Genesis 3:6 And when the woman saw that the tree was good for food, and that it was pleasant to the eyes, and a tree to be desired to make one wise, she took of the fruit thereof, and did eat, and gave also unto her husband with her, and he did eat.

2.) – T-or-F- But his wife looked back from behind him, and she became a pillar of salt. That golden city looked nice.

3.) – T-or-F- In Genesis 25:29-34 Did the red pottage look good enough for Esau to sell his birthright to Jacob?

4.) – T-or-F- In 2 Samuel 11:2-27 Verse 2 Did King David look upon the beautiful woman, Bathsheba, the wife of Uriah?

5.) – T-or-F- In Ecclesiastes 12:6 Are we not important to God that, Verse 6 reads. 5, 6 or ever the silver cord be loosed, or the golden bowl be broken, or the pitcher be broken at the fountain, or the wheel broken at the cistern. Verse 7 then shall the dust return to the earth as it was; and the spirit shall return unto God who gave it?

6.) – T-or-F- In Isaiah 28:16 did the Lord God say, he would lay a foundation stone, a tried stone, a precious corner stone, a sure foundation so he that believeth shall not make haste. 16-18 we shall not go to hell?

7.) – T-or-F- In Matthew 19:16-21 Did Jesus tell the rich man, that he could have treasure in heaven, if he followed him?

8.) – T-or-F- in Matthew 27:1-9 Did Judas know the thirty pieces of silver, wasn't worth the betrayal of innocent blood?

9.) – T-or-F- In Matthew 6:19-33 does Jesus tell them not to lay up treasures on earth, because ye must first seek the kingdom of God, and all these things shall be added unto you?

10.) – T-or-F- In Acts 5:1-10 verse 3 But Peter said, Ananias, why hath Satan filled thou heart to lie to the holy Ghost, and to keep back part of the price of the land?

11.) 1 Samuel 15:1-21 – T-or-F- verse 21 But the people took of the spoil, sheep and oxen, the chief of the things which should have been destroyed.

12.) – T-or-F- Jeremiah 10:1-5 verse 4 they deck it with silver and gold, they fasten it with nails and hammers, that it moves not.

13.) – T-or-F- In Luke 16:19-25 Did Jesus say Lazarus and the rich man had riches, one on earth and other with Abraham's bosom?

14.) – T-or-F- Did Mary in John 12:1-8 verse 3 take a pound of ointment of spikenard, very costly, and anointed the feet of Jesus and wiped his feet with her hair?

15.) – T-or-F- 4, 5 Did Judas want the cost of the ointment of 300 pence?

16.) – T-or-F- In 2 Peter 3:7-13 Is the Earth and elements and all the works therein, shall melt with fervent heat, dissolved?

17.) – T-or-F- In Revelation 21:21 is God going to destroy the old earth and heavens and make a new earth and heaven and New Jerusalem?

18.) – T-or-F- Are your treasures here on earth, to build this earth?

19.) – T-or-F- Are you building the kingdom of God, that shall never be destroyed, by the great coming of the Lord Jesus?

20.) – T-or-F- In Luke 12:15-21 verse 21 Is he that layeth up treasure for himself and is not he rich toward God?

21.) – T-or-F- Luke 18:22-30 Did Jesus say everlasting life is more valuable than money?

22.) – T-or-F- In James 1:12 Did it say he shall receive the crown of life?

23.) – T-or-F- In Job 28:1-20 Is wisdom more valuable than all riches of the world?

24.) – T-or-F- John 3:1-10 Even thou Nicodemus was a Master, a ruler, a Pharisee, a Rabbi, did Jesus tell him, he had to be born of water and Spirit, or he could not enter into the Kingdom of God?

Chapter 8

Diamond or Fake

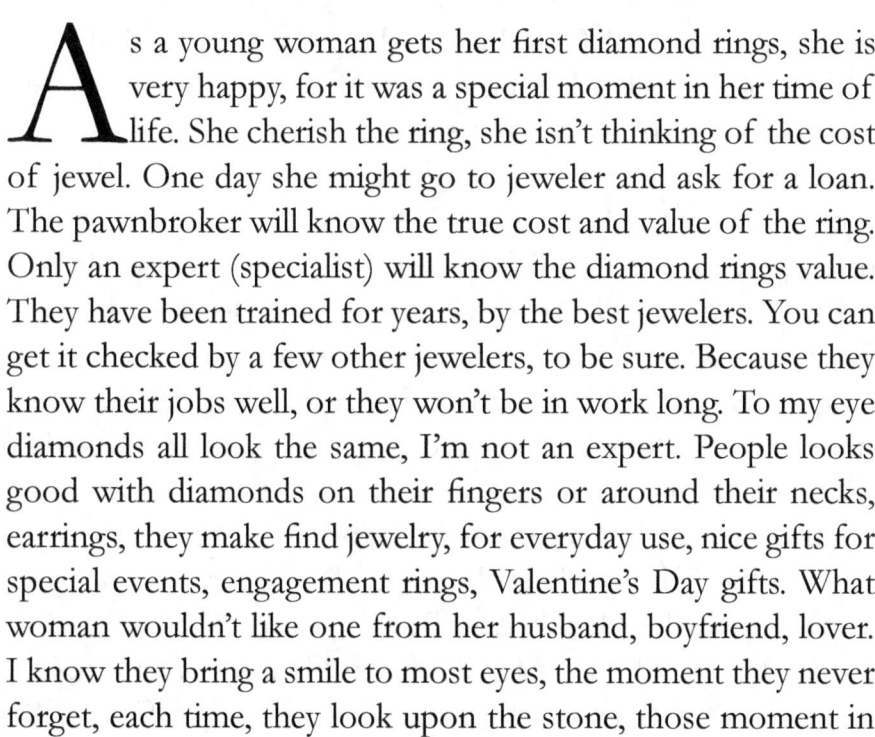

As a young woman gets her first diamond rings, she is very happy, for it was a special moment in her time of life. She cherish the ring, she isn't thinking of the cost of jewel. One day she might go to jeweler and ask for a loan. The pawnbroker will know the true cost and value of the ring. Only an expert (specialist) will know the diamond rings value. They have been trained for years, by the best jewelers. You can get it checked by a few other jewelers, to be sure. Because they know their jobs well, or they won't be in work long. To my eye diamonds all look the same, I'm not an expert. People looks good with diamonds on their fingers or around their necks, earrings, they make find jewelry, for everyday use, nice gifts for special events, engagement rings, Valentine's Day gifts. What woman wouldn't like one from her husband, boyfriend, lover. I know they bring a smile to most eyes, the moment they never forget, each time, they look upon the stone, those moment in time, thoughts return. One for engagement, on for marriage, anniversary's special gift.

The Bible tells us in, Revelation 21:18-21 all those Jewels. These earthly stones will all melt away some day, but those in the New Jerusalem, shall remain forever, who is looking for those precious stones, which will never fade away, no, not ever. So we must all look forward to that special kingdom of gold and stones, so much more value, than these diamonds and treasures. Where your treasures are, is where your heart is, earthly or heavenly. Some people look for earthly treasures, but Jesus said, look for heavenly treasures, that last forever.

Then all must be born of water and spirit, like Apostles Peter and Paul, plus all those Apostles preached and gave their lives for. God, made a way for us all, 1st John 3:16 Hereby perceive the love of God, because he laid down his life for us, and we ought to lay down our lives for the Brethren. They all died for us. Acts started the true church of God, those 120 men and women shock the world, we need preachers like that today, preachers who will humble their selves, lay their pride down, and preach like Saint Peter and Apostle Paul, the real doctrine salvation. Even the Devil knowns, Jesus is the One True God, who gave up His life for us, so we can have Eternal Life. If we are told to do all things in Jesus' name, then why not Baptize in Jesus' lovely name, if our sins are pardoned in Jesus' name, then why not obey the Apostles, diamond, real doctrine truth salvation, don't settle for fake watered down. Jesus is calling His lost sheep, hear the Master, come to the light, don't stay in the Devil's Angel's light, he came to kill, steal, and destroy us all, tricking preachers is his work of words. Just like he tricked Eve and Adam, in the Garden of Eden. Old devil, laughs at Preachers today, they are blinded by his light, then they lead the blind to hell, it's time to awake world, come to Jesus' light, just like the Early Apostle's first true salvation. Acts 2:38-42 Apostle Peter preached that day 120 plus 3,000 souls were saved, Apostle Paul lead many to doctrine truth. He wrote most of the New Testament, to warn us all, about false preachers, would come preaching false, fake truth. Preachers don't be upset or angry, Jesus is trying to get you all, to his light, he has great plans for you today, to feed the blind lead them into his light, devil has blinded his people, way too long. Who will work for Jesus, why there is still time, for Salvation.

What are we truly looking for in this old life? No one can take nothing with them, the kings of old, their things, was burying along with them in death, but others dug them up. As the old saying goes, we came in this world wearing nothing, the same way out of this world, someone else dresses us at death. Insurance, Life insurance isn't cheap, everybody needs life insurance. Every one of us is going to the grave, like, Ecclesiastes 3:1, 2 1 To everything there is a season, and a time to every purpose under the heaven. 2 A time to be born, and a time to die: well that says everything about earth life. We know we need life insurance. Now please let us go to Eternal Life Insurance, in John 3:3-5 Jesus answered and said unto him, verily, verily, (in every truth) (truly confidently) I say unto thee, except a man (be born again), he cannot see the kingdom of God. Verse 4, Nicodemus saith unto him, how can a man be born when he is old? Can he enter the second time into his mother's womb and be born? 5 Jesus answered, verily, verily, I say unto thee, except a man be born of (water and of the Spirit) he cannot enter into the kingdom of God. 6 that which is born of the flesh is flesh, and that which is born of the Spirit is Spirit. Now we see two births.

Let's go now to Acts 2:37 Now when they heard this, they were pricked (to pierce the heart) (remorse) the dog's ears (ready for sound). Ready for knowledge, want to know the truth, the right way, and said unto Peter and to the (rest of the Apostles,) men and brethren what shall we do? Verse 38 then Peter said unto them, Repent and be (baptized) every one of you in the name of (Jesus Christ) for the (remission) (forgive, pardon) of sins, and ye shall receive the gift of the Holy Ghost. This gift is like a diamond gift. It's real, not fake like those water down false preachers has spoken for years. Just believe, you're saved, sadly they are lost, till there born again, as John 3:3-5 and Acts 2:38-42. If Jesus said, except a man be born of water and Spirit.

10:15 And how shall they preach, except they be sent? As it is written, how beautiful are the feet of them that preach the gospel of peace, and bring glad tidings of good things. 16 But they have not obeyed the gospel. For Esaias saith, Lord, who hath believed our report? 17 So then faith cometh by hearing, and hearing by the word of God. 18 But I say, have they not heard? Yes verily, their sound went into all the earth, and their words unto the ends of the world. Matthew 24:11 And many false prophets shall rise, and shall deceive (many). 14 And this gospel of the kingdom shall be preached in all the world for a witness unto all nations; and then shall the end come. Mark 10:15 verily I say unto you, whosoever shall not receive the kingdom of God, as a little child, he shall not enter there in. Luke 11:13 If ye then, being evil, know how to give good gifts unto your children; how much more shall your heavenly Father give the Holy Spirit to them that ask him? Acts 2:37-42. 39 Promise is for all. James 3:8 But the tongue can no man tame; it is an unruly evil, full of deadly poison. 1 Corinthians 3:18

JESUS' APOSTLES - TRUE BORN AGAIN DOCTRINE

Let no man deceive himself. If any man among you seemeth to be wise in this world, let him become a fool. That he may be wise. 1 Corinthians 2:10 But God has revealed them unto us by his Spirit; for the Spirit searcheth all things, yea, the deep thing of God. Acts 8:16 (For as yet) he was fallen upon none of them; only they were baptized in the name of the Lord Jesus. 17 then laid they their hands on them, and they received the Holy Ghost. 18 And when Simon saw that through laying on of Apostle's hands the Holy Ghost was given, he offered them money, 19 saying give me also this power, that on whosoever I lay hands, he may receive the Holy Ghost. 20 But Peter said unto him, They money perish with thee, because thou hast thought that the gift of God maybe purchased with money. Acts 2:38-42. 39 For the promise is unto you, and to your children and to all that are afar off, even as many as the Lord our God shall call. The Lord our God, is calling us all, even in these a far off days. God is pouring out the Holy Ghost gift, to all who wants the Spirit. Choose this day, to be born of the water and the Spirit, as those men and women chose on Pentecostal Day, 120 plus 3,000 souls were added. Acts 26:18 To open their eyes, and turn them from darkness to light, and from the power of Satan (devil) unto God, that they may receive forgiveness of sins, and inheritance among them which as sanctified by faith that is in me.

There is no shame in not knowing the truth doctrine salvation words. Nicodemus was a ruler, a Pharisee, ruler of the Jews, knew not. Apostle Paul, didn't know the Doctrine Truth Salvation, till he was taught, the way, then he taught so many more, he wrote to warn all , about the light, true light or the world, Jesus. Sure he thought he was right, but, Jesus knew his heart, just like preacher today. He knows your hearts, he is waiting on you preachers, come, to preach, the true doctrine, you already know the Bible, now he wants us all to lead the blind into His light, get out of devil's darkness, light. Matthew 24:11 And many false prophets shall rise, and shall deceive many. Luke 11:13 If ye then, being evil, know how to give good gifts unto your children: how much more shall your heavenly father give the Holy Spirit to them that ask him? Luke 12:12 For the Holy Ghost shall teach you in the same hour what ye ought to say. Acts 2:28-29 read the words Apostle Peter told all to do, to the last far off days. Apostle Paul spoke the True Doctrine in Acts 19:1-6. Paul rebaptized those 12 again into Jesus' lovely name and laid his hands unto them. The Holy Ghost came on them; and they spake with tongues, and prophesied. Do you believe the Apostle's True Doctrine? Will you become saved a born again Christian, just like the Early first Church saints did? Search the Scriptures: for in them (ye think) ye have eternal life: and they are they which testify of me. John 5:29-40 And ye will not come to me, that ye might have life. Acts 2:38-42 For all. Saint Peter called the 120 plus 3,000 souls, in Acts 2:38-42. Jesus said upon you, I will build my church. Matthew 16:16-19 What church are you really in today? Apostle's churches today still preach Saint Peter's Acts 2:38-42. The very same Doctrine. Real or Fake, you must study for your own Salvation, eternal life. Revelation 20:6, 14 Second death, for the lost souls.

True (T) or False (F) Questions

1.) – T. or. F. In the Book of Acts, do you believe the Apostle's started the First Original Church, on the Day of Pentecost?

2.) – T. or. F. Have you followed the Apostle's baptism, in Jesus' name for the remission of your sins?

3.) – T. or. F. Did you receive the Gift of the Holy Ghost by speaking in tongues, as in, Acts 19:1-6?

4.) – T. or. F. In 2 Corinthians 13:5 Have you checked your Doctrine and Faith, to see if it's the real doctrine truth?

5.) – T. or. F. In Jude 1:3 Did Jude, Jesus' brother tell us about the common salvation, to contend for the faith of the saints?

6.) In Timothy 4:1, 13-16 was Apostle Paul warning us all, in the latter times (end time) about seducing spirits and doctrines of devils?

7.) – T. or. F. In Philippians 2:12 does Paul tell us to work out your own salvation with fear and trembling?

8.) – T. or. F. Does Apostle Paul, tell us, in Ephesians 2:20-22 19 starts out to say of saints, the Apostles and Prophets, and Jesus Christ himself being the chief corner stone?

9.) – T. or. F. In Corinthians 2:10 does it say the Spirit searcheth all things, yes the deep things of God?

10.) – T. or. F. As you read Romans 9:15 Did God say to Moses, I will have mercy on whom I have mercy on?

11.) – T. or. F. In Romans 8:5-11 Is that same Spirit that raised Jesus, from the dead, in you, to quicken your mortal body?

12.) – T. or. F. In Acts 26:14-18 Are you willing to come out of the power of Satan, into Jesus' light, as Apostle Paul spoke of?

13.) – T. or. F. In Acts 26:26-29 Are you almost persuades to become a true Christian, like those in Acts 2:38-42 souls added?

14.) – T. or. F. Are you, your family also willing to search Apostolic true Doctrine Churches out for your own salvations, with fear and trembling?

15.) – T. or. F. In Revelation 20:10-14 Are you in Book of Life, or second death?

Chapter 9

Counterfeit Money

As I was once a little boy, I didn't know the money things. When I was one or two years old, I couldn't go to the store, to buy candy, nor toys, we were given coins, candy, from our families. Then at a certain age we played with play money, coins, all of us. Once we understood the real value, worth of a dollar or quarter, dime. We could go to the store or bank, and do what we needed. Now like coin collectors, or pawn-brokers, can give you the right figure. Because they know the price of money, coins, that's their job. Then we talk about stock markets, the buying and selling. Most people don't understand how easy it could be, once you get started into that field of knowledge and true understanding. We let those trained, to do such things for us, smart, right. Sure we all have an ideal of small money matters, but, it's hard to figure the big bucks things, because we pay them to be fair. If I had a counterfeit dollar and a real dollar in my hand, sadly, I couldn't tell the difference, I wasn't taught, no chance. The Bible is the hardest thing to figure and truly understand. It was writing by the prophets, disciples, Apostles, those were the best expert in those things. 2 Peter 1:20, (21) For the prophecy came no in old time by the will of man; but holy men of God spake as they were moved by the Holy Ghost.

1:20 knowing this first, that no prophecy of the scripture is of any private interpretation. The Apostle's in Acts 2:38-42 showed the real doctrine truth. Nothing like the counterfeit, water down Gospel, that preacher today, just believe, have faith, trust your preacher, no works, just trust. Well I thank God, for these Apostolic Church preachers today, that are in these last or end time days, that Apostle Peter and Apostle Paul, said would preach to us far off generations, the Apostles Doctrine. Please get your dictionary down and read these words, go to the page, (Apostolic) of or relating to an Apostle or to the New Testament Apostles.

Of or relating to a succession of (spiritual authority) from the Apostles. Saint Peter in Acts 2:38-42 said this is for all, who God calls, even to (us) who are a far off. Not just then. Every last one of us shall stand by ourselves in front of the great white throne. Alone, no lawyer, no preacher, before God. Revelation 20:11-14 Heaven or second death, your choice, you, your family, friends, church, brothers and sisters. In John 3:3-5 Nicodemus didn't understand, that you had to be born of water and the spirit, then Jesus explained to him. Acts 8, 9 Both Chapters tells how Apostle Paul, was born again not just by faith, but, by Jesus' name Only baptized, then spoke in tongues, the way Saint Peter's words in Acts 2:38-42 was given to all, then and now, yes, these Apostolic Preachers, in churches today. No halfway, no I thought, not preacher told me, no lawyer, no second chance, just heaven or that second death, meant for devil. Oh, how sad, please don't wait to the Great White Throne. Take time today, don't wait till tomorrow, it isn't promised, to no man, no woman, today is what each one has, time is short.

You can search the Scriptures in your Bible, the web, or call an Apostolic Church preacher, anytime, your Eternal life, take an hour. Every hour you have left, depends on your humble choice today. Some preachers sound really great, Nicodemus was a ruler, Saul or Apostle Paul thought and was taught, but they both were wrong, till taught the born again true way, water and Spirit. In Acts 8:13-19 He wasn't saved, even was baptized in Jesus' name, had faith, saw others receive the tongue spoken gift of the Holy Ghost filling, perished he was, read this, please. Let the Expert Apostolic, help you with Eternal life, check all things. The life you save, might be yours or your family's, or brothers and sisters in your church, the ones you love in Christ Jesus.

Chapter -9- Questions True (T) or False (F)

1.) – T-or-F- In 1 Kings 22:19 was the Lord's throne, the only one?

2.) – T-or-F- Did Satan say, in Isaiah 14:12-14 and cast down from heaven because he wanted to build a throne above the throne of God?

3.) – T-or-F- in John 8:12 did Jesus say, I am the Light of the world?

4.) – T-or-F- in Acts 26 did Apostle Paul say that he was to deliver the Gentiles (us) out of the darkness of the power of Satan, into the light?

5.) – T-or-F- In 2 Corinthians 11:13-15 didn't Apostle Paul, say that Satan and the false apostles, would also be ministers, also transformed as the ministers of light and righteousness, deceitful workers?

6.) – T-or-F- In Acts 2:1-4, 16, 21, 36-42 did all these brothers and sisters speak in Tongues when the Holy Ghost filled them?

7.) – T-or-F- In Acts 8:12, 13 did Simon the sorcery believe, and even as he was baptized in Jesus' name, yet he didn't receive the Holy Ghost was he saved?

8.) – T-or-F- In Acts 10:34, 35-48 Did they speak in tongues, when they received the gift of the Holy Ghost?

9.) – T-or-F- In Acts 13:46, 47 did Apostle Paul say he was to be a light to the Gentiles, for salvation to the end of the earth?

10.) – T-or-F- In Timothy 2:3, 4 does it say that God, wants all men, to come into the knowledge of the truth?

11.) – T-or-F- In Luke 7:29 did he say they were all baptized by John?

12.) – T-or-F- In Luke 16:25-29 does it say, they have Moses and the prophets, let them hear them?

13.) – T-or-F- In Acts 2:38-42 what Apostle Peter said to them, their children and (all) a far off, do you believe the true doctrine?

14.) – T-or-F- In Acts 8:1 did Saul persecute the church of God, by putting away all those who preached, Apostle Peter's Acts 2:38-42 true gospel?

15.) – T-or-F- Do you believe those Saints of the First church in Acts taught the born again Salvation, as in John 3:3-5 water and Spirit?

16.) – T-or-F- Can you know for sure your name is written in Revelation 20:15 the Book of Life?

Chapter 10

Forerunners

Matthew 3:1-8 In those days came John the Baptist, preaching in the wilderness of Judea. 2 And saying: Repent ye for the kingdom of heaven is at hand. 3 for this is he that was spoken by the prophet Esaias, saying, the voice or one crying in the wilderness, prepare ye the way of the Lord, make his path straight. 6 And were baptized of him in Jordan (confessing their sins). 8 Bring forth therefore fruits meet for repentance. In the Webster Dictionary. Fore-Run-Ner- One that goes before to give notice of the approach of others. John was preparing the way. We read how John was only Baptizing for repent, turn away from sins. Acts 19:1-6. 3 And he said unto them, Unto what then were ye baptized? 4 Then said Paul, John verily baptized with the baptism of repentance, saying unto the people, that they should believe of him which should come after him, that is Christ Jesus. 5 When they heard this, they were baptized in the name of the Lord Jesus. 6 And when Paul laid his hands on them; and they spake with tongues. Repent is the first step, we read in Acts 2:38 Peter told them to repent and be baptized every one of you in the name of Jesus Christ for the (remission) – (forgive, pardon) of sins, and ye shall receive the gift of the Holy Ghost. 39 For the promise is unto you, and to your children, (a male or female offspring, son, daughter, generation to come) and to all that are a far off, even as many as the Lord our God shall call. Today's Preachers say, just believe and you're saved, faith is good, but Jesus said in John 3:3-5 and Mark 16:16 He that believeth (and) is baptized shall be saved; but he that believed not shall be damned. Damn-loss- to condemn (esp.) to hell, curse. Hell- netherworld to exist. 1 Peter 3:21 The like figure wore unto even baptism doth also now save us (not the putting away of the filth of the flesh, but the answer of a good conscience towards God,) by the resurrection of Jesus Christ. James 2:20 but wilt thou know, o vain man, that faith without works is dead? 2:24 ye see then how that by works a man is justified, and not by faith only. 2:26 For as the body without the spirit is dead, so faith without works is dead also.

Saint Peter taught the true doctrine, not the John Baptism first way. Repent, turn away from your old sinful life, was the first step. He didn't stop there, he went on to say, Baptize in Jesus' name. Most important step was, to get the Holy Ghost, tongue Spirit. Apostle Paul, said he spoke more in tongues, than everyone else. He could tell when someone, received the Holy Ghost gift. Simon the Sorcerer, had faith, and was baptized in Jesus' name, but he thought the Holy Ghost, after he saw others receive gift of the Holy Ghost could be bought with money, and give to his own choice.

So many brothers and sisters, think they are born again, oh how I pray for those, because they were blinded by the devil's tricks. Apostles, warned us all, how the wolves would come and steal, the true doctrine salvation. Saint Peter said this was the way for us all. Thank God, those Apostolic preachers today, far off, last days, do have the born again Doctrine, like those 120 men and women and 3,000 they laugh about those Holy Rollers today, they still speak in tongues. The Jesus' name Baptism, still remission sins, is so very important. Repent, was the first step, Jesus' death, burial, then resurrection. The Great White Throne, don't truth no one, search the scriptures. 1st Corinthians 2:10 But God has revealed them unto us by his Spirit, for the Spirit searcheth all things, yes, the (deep) things of God. 1st Corinthians 14:18 Paul's words. I thank my God, I speak with tongues more than ye all. Apostle Paul once destroyed those Early Church brothers and sisters, who taught Saint Peter's Doctrine True Salvation. I hope your hearts and minds, follow those Early Doctrine, first Saints, King Agrippa. Acts 26:27, 28 I know thou believed. 28 Then Agrippa said unto Paul, (almost) thou persuades me to be a Christian. (Almost) Please search the Scriptures, don't be another King Agrippa lost soul.

Chapter -10- Questions – True (T) or False (F)

1.) – T-or-F- In Exodus 7:1 did the Lord say unto Moses, I have made thee a god to Pharaoh?

2.) – T-or-F- In Mark 1:44 did Jesus say, do thy cleansing things Moses commanded?

3.) – T-or-F- In Deuteronomy 6:4 did Moses say the Lord our God is one?

4.) – T-or-F- In Mark 12 did Jesus say in verse 29 the first of all the commandments is hear, O Israel: the Lord our God is one Lord?

5.) – T-or-F- In Luke 16:29-31 was Moses name, before the prophets?

6.) – T-or-F- And did the Sadducees speak about what Moses wrote in Luke 20:27, 28?

7.) – T-or-F- In John 7:16-24 Was Jesus speaking about Moses' laws?

8.) – T-or-F- In John 6:32, 33 Moses gave manna in the desert, then Jesus gave the bread from heaven, the true bread?

9.) – T-or-F- In Jonah 1:17 was Jonah in the belly of fish for 3 days and nights?

10.) In Luke 11:32 was Jesus preaching about Jonah's time?

11.) Luke 18:31-33 Did Jesus speak about the prophets had wrote?

12.) – T-or-F- In Romans 5:13, 14 Did it say death reigned from Adam to Moses even unto them that had not sinned after the similitude of Adam's transgression, who is the figure of him that was to come?

13.) – T-or-F- In Romans 8:6-11 Are we made alive by the Spirit of Christ, that same Spirit that raised Jesus from dead?

14.) – T-or-F- In Romans 9:15 was it said about Moses, from God, I will have mercy on whom I will have mercy?

15.) – T-or-F- In Hebrews 8:1-13 Was Moses, and Jesus, also both in first and second new covenant, one the law, second the Spirit?

16.) – T-or-F- In Matthew 8:17 that it might be fulfilled which was spoken by Esaias the prophet, saying, himself took our sins and bare our sickness?

17.) – T-or-F- In Matthew 12:39-41 didn't Jonas go into the wale 3 days and three nights, in the heart of the earth?

18.) – T-or-F- In Luke 7:29 Where they baptized with the baptism of John?

19.) – T-or-F- in Acts 2:37-42 Did Apostle Peter tell them to get baptized, in Jesus' name for the remission of sins.

20.) – T-or-F- In Acts 19:1-6 Did Apostle Paul tell them thy same words as Acts 2:38?

21.) – T-or-F- In Acts 5:29-32 did Peter and the other Apostles say, we ought to obey God rather than men?

Chapter 11

Jesus' Powerful Authority

As I start this Chapter, I want all to understand what name God chose for Himself, from Exodus 6:3. And I appeared unto Abraham, unto Isaac, and unto Jacob, by the name of God Almighty, but by my name JEHOVAH was I not known to them. Isaiah 9:6 For unto us a child is born, unto us a son is given, and the government (authority) shall be upon his shoulder; and his name shall be called Wonderful, Counselor, the Mighty God, the Everlasting Father, the Prince of Peace. Matthew 28:18 and Jesus came and spake unto them, saying, All Power is given unto me in heaven and in earth. Revelation 1:10-18. 14 His head and hairs were white like world, as white as snow; and his eyes were as a flame of fire. 17 And when I saw him, I fell at his feet as dead. And he laid his right hand upon me, saying unto me, Fear not; I am the first and the last. Verse 18 I am he that liveth, and was dead; and have the keys of Hell and of death.

Scholars and Theologians, just like in Nicodemus and Apostle Paul's days, you all are very wise, but, this will not get you into the Kingdom of God. Matthew 15:9 But in vain they do worship me, teaching for (doctrines of men.) 1 Corinthians 1:19 For it is written, I Will destroy the wisdom of the wise, and will bring to nothing the understanding of the prudent. (Stupid) simple, lacking education. Acts 2:4-7 Those unlearned (Galileans) spake in other heard nation language. Acts 2:37-39 verse 37 what shall we do? Isaiah 9:6 the Mighty God, Everlasting Father. 12:2 Behold, God is my salvation; I will trust, and not be afraid. For the Lord JEHOVAH, is my salvation; I will trust, and not be afraid. For the Lord Jehovah, is my strength and my song; he also is become my salvation.

Mark 12:28 And one of the Scribes came, and having heard them reasoning together, and perceiving that he had answered them well, asked him, which is the first commandment of all? Verse 29 And Jesus answered him, the first of all the commandments is, Hear, O Israel, The Lord our God is one Lord. Acts 4:12 Neither is there Salvation in any other: for there is none other name under heaven given among men, whereby we must be saved. What name are you baptized into, Jesus? As I was watching T.V. a while back in February 2022, a deacon or a Bishop, spoke about Baptizing, people in his church the wrong way. His, words were, (We) Baptize in the name of (Father, son and Holy Ghost for the remission of your sins. We not I?

If the romans back in those days, took Jesus' lovely name, out of the Apostles Doctrine's Truth Salvation Baptism, we will correct that? Who will start baptizing their brothers and sisters the way that, those first Saints did? They laid their lives down for all, then, now, even in these far off latter, end times. Where are the brace brothers and sisters, till they do receive the same Holy Ghost, speaking in tongues likes 3,000 then. Are we able to baptism 3,000 today, like the Early Church did? It has been almost 2,000 years since that first outpouring of the holy Ghost filling, so many at one time, the Apostolic Churches today still does these wonderful things, pick up your phone, dial the churches, you will be surprised by their answers, call. Take your money, build bigger churches, your money can save more than just 3,000 souls in these far off end time days. Or do you like to be in the Dark Ages for 1900 more years, no. The time is now, to help these brothers and sisters, family, and friends, get the early Apostles Doctrine Truth Salvation. I want to write the Doctrine of those Early Apostle's Church in every language, I hope and pray to reach, China, North and South, knock down walls, break devil's hold on all churches. Donations to churches, to build the Kingdom of God, like those Saints started 2,000 years ago. Yes, to the Rapture of churches. When the Saints go marching in, I want these end time churches to bring millions, into those clouds with Jesus. Who will start the flock into the light with Jesus' baptism? What man or woman preacher, will preach like Saint Peter and Apostle Paul, done in those early first Church, Tongue speaking, Holy Ghost filled brothers and sisters, done for us all?

He quoted doing this for many years, he apologize for his mistakes on this. Yes just one words makes baptism very wrong, in all churches, these days. In Acts 2:38 then Peter said unto them, repent and be baptized every one of you in the name of (Jesus Christ) for the remission of your sins, and ye shall receive the gift of the Holy Ghost. Verse 39 For the Promise is unto you, and to your children, and to all that are a far off, even as many as the Lord our God shall call.

The Early Apostle's Church members obeyed those exact, accurate, correct words, when they baptized in the Book of Acts, then in 325 AD, the changes were made by, Justin Martyr, along with Augustine. Tertullian coined the term (Trinity), they decided that Jesus' name should be blotted out, removed from Baptism, then Constantine Baptized his entire arm in the words (Father, Son and Holy Ghost) He advised all that were baptized in (Jesus' name) to be rebaptized the same way. That old devil has laughed for 1600 years now, he is the father of lies. He came to kill, steal, and to destroy, God's perfect plan of salvation, where is Jesus' name in baptism today, thank God His Apostle (Apostolic Churches, are back in these far off days. The Original Apostle (Apostolic Churches) started back in 1914, there are churches everywhere, check the phonebooks, the newspapers, the web, it should take one hour of your time, to find things out. It's time to put old devil and his demons out of our churches. In Acts 2:38-42 3,000 souls were baptized, that special day. The whole way in Acts Book, tells how everyone was baptized into Jesus' lovely name, for the true way of remission for your sins. Internet, look all scriptures up, your eternal life, one hour is all it takes to search for your, family and friends, true salvation.

Apostle Paul warned us all, how the wolves would come to destroy the Original Apostle's True Salvation, everything is done in Jesus' lovely name, where is his lovely name now, today. 1600 years, is a long time in darkness, let's go to, let go to the light. Jesus is calling us, in these far off days, go back to true doctrine. Preachers Jesus wants all of you, he knows your pain, you lost many loved ones to the old devil's tricky lies, save yourself, from those sad lies of devil, Jesus' name Apostolic Churches, doors are wide open.

JESUS' APOSTLES - TRUE BORN AGAIN DOCTRINE

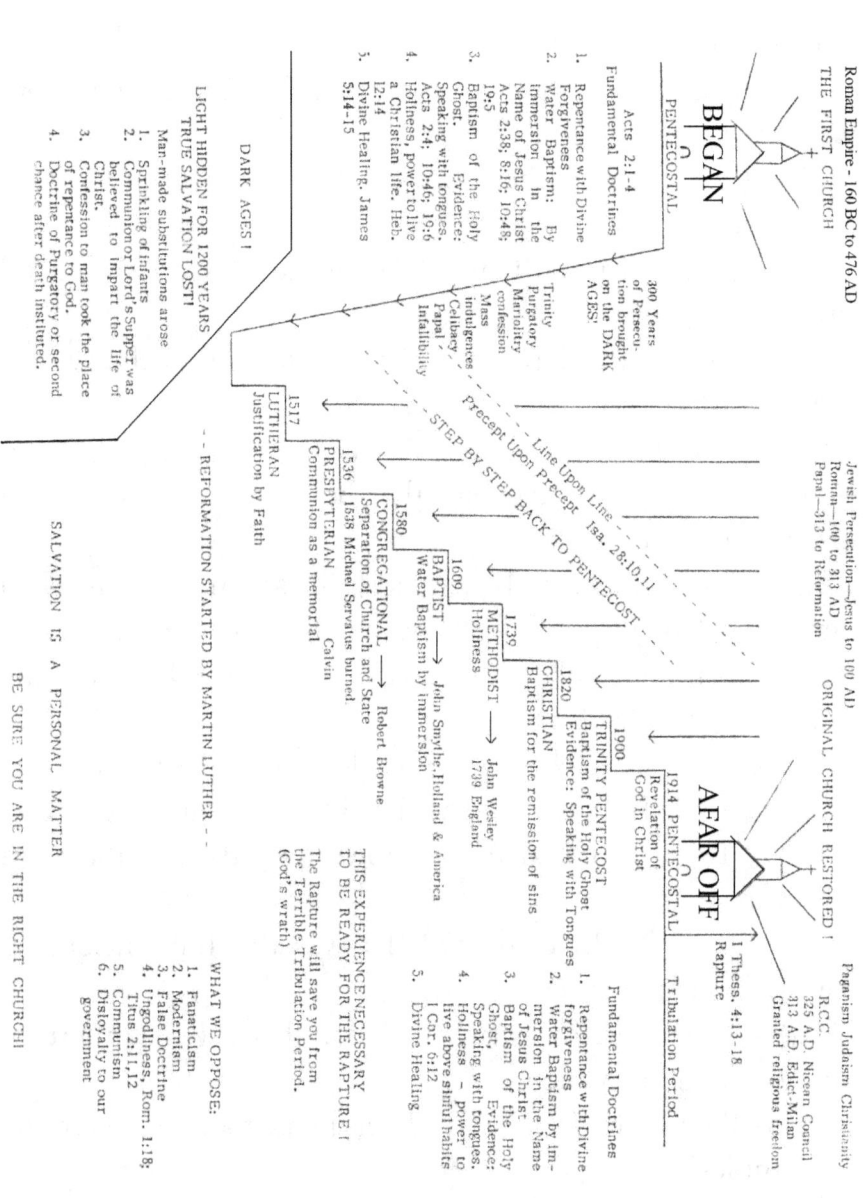

Chapter 11 – Jesus' Powerful Authority – Questions

True (T) or False (F)

1.) – T. or. F. In Matthew 1:21-25 Was Jesus to save us from our sins?

2.) – T. or. F. In Matthew 7:22-23 did they cast out devils in his name?

3.) – T. or. F. In Matthew 13:41 Did Jesus say I shall send forth my Angels?

4.) – T. or. F. In Matthew 28:18 Did Jesus say all power is given unto him in heaven and earth?

5.) – T. or. F. In Mark 2:5-11 Did they say only God can forgive sins, and did Jesus say that he the Son of Man hath power to forgive sins?

6.) – T. or. F. In Mark 16:17 Did Jesus say in my name shall they cast out devils, they shall speak with new tongues?

7.) – T. or. F. In Luke 10:17-20 Did Jesus give those seventy power over the devils in his name?

8.) – T. or. F. In Hebrews 4:8 did Jesus give them rest?

9.) – T. or. F. In Exodus 20:8-11 did the Lord give them rest?

10.) – T. or. F. In Isaiah 26:4 does it say trust in the Lord Jehovah?

11.) – T. or. F. In Daniel 7:9-10 Was this the Ancient of Days who sat?

12.) – T. or. F. In Zechariah 14:1-9 in that day shall there be one Lord and his name one?

13.) – T. or. F. In Malachi 1:11 Is his name today great among the Gentiles?

14.) – T. or. F. In Malachi 4:1-6 did the Lord say he was coming for that great and dreadful day?

15.) – T. or. F. In Matthew 3:11 does it say Jesus will baptize you with the Holy Ghost?

16.) – T. or. F. In Mark 15:17 Did Jesus say in my name they shall cast out devils?

17.) – T. or. F. In John 5:43 Did Jesus say I come in my Father's name and ye receive me not; if another come in his own name ye will receive him?

18.) – T. or. F. In John 10:30 Did Jesus say, I and my Father are one?

19.) – T. or. F. In John 13:1-44 Did Jesus speak to Lazarus, even after he was dead four days, and say come forth, did Lazarus, come a live?

20.) – T. or. F. In John 14:1-8 did Jesus say, you see me you see my father?

21.) – T. or. F. In John 14:13-18 did Jesus say he was the comforter Holy Ghost?

22.) – T. or. F. In John 17:1-26 Was Jesus saying in verse 6 I have manifested (showing) the works of God in body?

23.) – T. or. F. In Revelation 1:12-18 Did Jesus say, I am the first and the Last, verse 18 I am he that liveth and was dead, and behold, I am alive forevermore, and have the keys of hell and death?

24.) – T. or. F. In Deuteronomy 32:39, 40 Did God say, there is no god with him, and I kill and make a live?

25.) – T. or. F. In Matthew 7:21-23 Was Jesus saying at judgement day, depart from me, I never knew you?

26.) – T. or. F. In Revelation 20:11-15 was the books opened to God/

27.) – T. or. F. In Matthew 28:18 Does Jesus has all power in heaven and earth, as he said?

Chapter 12

In the New Jerusalem

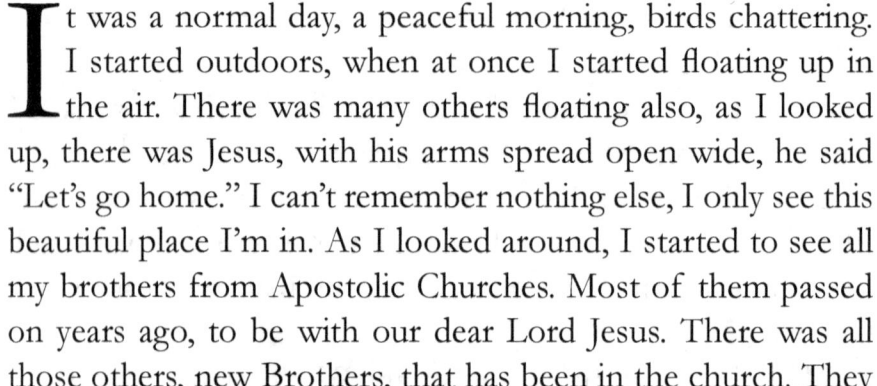

It was a normal day, a peaceful morning, birds chattering. I started outdoors, when at once I started floating up in the air. There was many others floating also, as I looked up, there was Jesus, with his arms spread open wide, he said "Let's go home." I can't remember nothing else, I only see this beautiful place I'm in. As I looked around, I started to see all my brothers from Apostolic Churches. Most of them passed on years ago, to be with our dear Lord Jesus. There was all those others, new Brothers, that has been in the church. They were with their families and friends, I never saw a lot of them, but they knew me, just like we was always together in our lives.

As I started walking around, I felt so good and healthy, like I was 21. I came to this river of pure water, as clear as crystal, coming out of the throne of God, I looked into the water, I saw a young man, me. I look so different, nothing like I looked all my whole life long. I thought I was dreaming for hours, but slowly I knew I was home. After I found Jesus, then I praised and worshipped him for a long time. Then I walked around for a spell, I heard others talking, there was Moses, Elias, with Jesus, talking and laughing like they were always home. Slowly, I looked around Jonah was telling all about the Big Fish story. Next I saw Noah pointing towards the rainbow around the throne of God. Looking around I saw King David playing his golden harp, to please the Lord. Oh, what a time I was having, I couldn't stop seeing so many new faces who looked my way. There came Saint Peter, he was pointing at those great high wall and twelve gates of the tribes of Israel. Then Apostle Paul stood there looking at the foundations of the Apostles. Then Apostle Paul stood there looking at the foundations of the Apostles. Slowly I looked around and saw those High walls of the city Revelations describes in verse 21:19-21. So many different Jewels and stones. I once saw man made homes and castles, that sold for millions of dollars. Here is my home, Jesus built and prepared it for every one of us. The humble shall enter, those born again, John 3:3-5 those I was blessed to hear the Master's calling his sheep home. At first, I said to the brother, I was baptized once, that is enough.

I didn't like his words, that I wasn't saved, that I had to be baptized again into water, in Jesus' lovely name, then I speak in tongues, filled by Holy Ghost. I was mad and didn't understand the True Apostle Peter's Salvation way. Yes, I rejected his words, over and over, to a month or so later. Then one day, I heard Jesus' calling, I was baptized into that lovely name of Jesus, for the remission of my sins, I had so many more, than I could count in a week, I was so glad that those sins was washed away, forever, oh what joy and peace I had I saw about 20 men going down in water, in Jesus' lovely name. Some came up speaking in different tongues, sadly I did not, then I knew I need it that gift of tongues giving Holy Ghost Eternal life. So I recall that day, it's my son's birthday, October 1st. For the next 2 weeks I prayed harder, finally one night, I prayed 45 minutes, my tongue started moving by its own power. It felt like a doctor or nurse was moving it, then different words came out, and words I'd never heard before in my life time. I was afraid, frightened a lot, so I stopped, sometimes when I pray, I speak in tongues for minutes, once for hours. God know all our thoughts and prayers, this is why, we must pray in the Spirit, tongues he hears. Sure, it was for those First Early Apostle's church brothers and sisters. Acts 2:38-42 says, for them and their children and all a far off. Well, your preacher don't believe that, nor does your family or friends, then read in Revelation 20:1-15 verse 6 blessed and Holy is he that hath part in the first resurrection on such the (second death no power), but they shall be priests of God and of Christ, and shall reign with him a thousand years. Revelation 20:9 And they went up on the breadth of the earth, and compassed the camp of the Saints about, and the beloved city (New Jerusalem); and fire came down from God out of heaven and devoured them. Where on this day, shall you, family, friends, brothers and sisters, and those preachers, who rejected God's True Salvation. Will you be in the New Jerusalem, or outside of those great walls? What is one hour of your life, to search those scriptures, don't trust man's words.

Chapter -12- In the New Jerusalem – Questions- True (T) or False (F)

1.) – T. or. F. In Daniel 7:13 And there was given him dominion, and glory, and a kingdom, that all people, nations, and languages, should serve him: his dominion is an everlasting dominion, which shall not pass away, and his kingdom that which shall not be destroyed?

2.) – T. or. F. In Hebrews 11:6-10 Abraham, verse 10, For he looked for a city which hath foundations, whose builder and make is God?

3.) – T. or. F. In Matthew 25:34 Then shall the king say unto them on the right hand, come, ye blessed of my Father, inherit the kingdom prepared for you from the foundation of the world?

4.) – T. or. F. Did Jesus say in, John 14: 1-6 verse 2 In my Father's house are many mansions: if it were not so, I would have told you, I go to prepare a place for you. 3 and if I go and prepare a place for you, I will come again, and receive you unto myself, that where I am, there ye may be also?

5.) – T. or. F. In Daniel 2:44 did it say, God shall make a kingdom, that shall last forever?

6.) – T. or. F. In Matthew 19:28 did Jesus say when he sits on his throne of glory, ye also shall sit upon twelve thrones, judging the nations?

7.) – T. or. F. In Mark 8:36 Did Jesus say, for what shall it profit a man, if he shall gain the whole world, and lost his own soul?

8.) – T. or. F. In Mark 12:25 Did Jesus say when we rise from the dead, we will be as the angels which are in heaven?

9.) – T. or. F. In Luke 9:30, 21 did Jesus appear in glory with Moses and Elias?

10.) – T. or. F. In John 3:3-5 did Jesus say except you be born of water and Spirit, he cannot see the kingdom of God?

11.) – T. or. F. In Romans 14:7-12 verse 9 did it say in this verse for to this end Christ both died, and rose, and revived, that he might be Lord both of the dead and living?

12.) – T. or. F. In Revelation 21:1-27 is a new heaven and earth, then a Holy city the New Jerusalem coming down from God out of heaven?

13.) – T. or. F. In Revelation 22:1-21 does it tell us about our new home?

14.) – T. or. F. In 1 Corinthians 15:40-52 does it say in a twinkling of an eye?

Chapter 13

Those Who Rejected the True Doctrine

Every one of us from Adam and Eve was born in this world. All of us started to learn the simple basic things in life. First, we were spanked to get us breath in our lungs. Next fed by bottle of milk, then solid food, laughing, crying, talking, walking, then taught by family, friends, of course teachers, preachers. As we look towards the skies we see, sun, moon, star and clouds. Then sometimes that nice rainbow, with so many colors in them. The Bible tells us where these things came from, our God. Now so may say, there isn't no God, but I say, let them try to make something out of nothing, no one yet, has done this. The Bible starts out in the Garden of Eden, where he made man out of the dust, then took a rib, to form Eve.

We all know about the trees in that garden, how the serpent, old devil, beguiled Eve and Adam, to eat the forbidden fruit, that God command not. Beguile (to deceive) like the devil told Eve, ye shall not surely die: But ye know about good and evil.

That deceiving devil brought death to us all. Adam and Eve lived a good long life, but sadly, they died, and all others to the end of time shall go to the dust, where Adam and Eve came from.

Next, the world became so sinful on the Earth, so good washed away all sin, by the Flood (water), except Noah and seven others, of his family members. Genesis 9:11-13 God made the covenant with the rainbow, not to destroy with water. Then we go to (Moses) the one who wrote the first five books in the Bible, he was moved by the Holy Ghost to write all things. In Exodus 2:10 –He was named (Moses). Exodus is the second book of Moses. Numbers 21:5-9, verse 5 And the people spake against God and Moses, verse 6 And the (Lord) sent fiery serpents among the people, and they bit the people and much people died. Verse 8 And the Lord said unto Moses, make thee a fiery serpent and set it upon a pole: and it shall come to pass, that everyone that is bitten when he beheld the serpent of brass, he lived.

The fifth book of Moses, Deuteronomy 6:4 Hear, O Israel; the Lord our God is one Lord. 32:39 See now that I, even I, am he, and there is no god with me: I kill, and I make alive; I wound, and I heal; neither is there any that can deliver out of my hand. Isaiah 9:6 The mighty God, everlasting father. John 1:10 He was in the world and the world was made by him and the world knows him not. 3:14 And as Moses lifted up the serpent in the wilderness, even so must the son of man be lifted up. Jesus took all sin on that cross.

1st John 3:16 Hereby we perceive (know) the love of God, because he laid down his life for us; and we ought to lay down our lives for the brethren. Dear Brothers and Sisters God (Lord) is the Father of all creation, so if (He) makes a body for (Himself), he is the Father of that body. God alone, gave his life as a man, for every sin in the world. One God, just one Throne, just one name, Jesus was God Himself in Human Form, not two gods, nor three, Just He. God's name is Jehovah, do we all agree with Exodus 6:3. Zechariah 14:4-12 verse 9 And the Lord shall be King over all the Earth in that day shall there be one Lord, and his name one. Daniel 7:9 I beheld till the thrones were cast down, and the Ancient of days did sit, whose garment was white as snow, and the hair of his head like the pure wool: His throne was like the fiery flame, and his wheels as burning fire. Verse 10 a fiery stream issued and came forth form before him; thousands, thousands ministered unto him, and ten thousand time ten thousand stood before him; the judgment was set, and the books were opened.

Acts 2:38-42, 8:13-20, 10:34, 43-48, 11:15-21, 18:24, 25, 19:1-6, 20:28, 26:13-19 verse 29 Then Agrippa said unto Paul, (almost) thou persuades me to be a Christian. 1st Corinthians 10:9 They tempted Christ. 1 Corinthians 14:39 Wherefore, brethren, covet to prophesy, and forbid not to speak with tongues. 2 Corinthians 11:13-15 Satan transformed into an angel. Dear brothers and sisters, I am (Jesus) within my body and Spirit. Let the Bible speak for us. 2 Corinthians 13:6 Examine yourselves, whether (ye) be in the faith; prove yourselves, how that Jesus Christ is in you, except (ye) be reprobates. (a person for ordained to damnation) (bad person). Luke 22:31, 32 31 And the Lord said, Simon, Simon, behold Satan hath desired to have (you), that he may sift you as wheat. 32 But I have prayed for thee, that thy faith fail not; and when thou art converted, strengthen thy brethren. Acts 10:33, 34 33 Immediately therefore I sent to thee; and thou hast done well. Now hear all things that are commandment of God. 34 Then Peter opened his mouth, and said, of a truth, I perceive that God is no respecter of persons. (worthy or respect) respect or difference between. God chooses whosoever He wills. I'm a born again Christian, the one same (Spirit) fillings as Saint Peter, Apostle Paul, and all brother and sisters from Acts 2:38-42. Even to the (far off days) in time God used a donkey (ass) to save a man's life once. Numbers 22:21-38 The words that God puts in my mouth (I shall speak). So if God used a (ass) once to speak, you must believe, that he can you a born again Christian who didn't reject the truth. Saint Peter's Acts 2:38-42

Chapter -13- Those Who Rejected the True Doctrine

Questions – True (T) or False (F)

1.) – T. or. F. in Genesis 4:2-7 did Cain have no respect for God?

2.) – T. or. F. In Genesis 6:1-13 did they obey God's grace in Noah's ark days?

3.) – T. or. F. In Genesis 18:16-33 and in Genesis 19:24-29 did God find ten righteous within the city, before he destroyed Sodom and Gomorrah with brimstone and fire from heaven?

4.) – T. or. F. In Exodus 12:21-30 did Pharaoh reject God's command to let the children of Israel go?

5.) – T. or. F. In Numbers 21:5-9 did God destroy those who spoke against God and Moses, with fiery serpents/

6.) – T. or. F. In 1 Samuel 15:21-24 did Saul lose his king's crown because he rejected the word of God?

7.) – T. or. F. In 2 Samuel 12:1-9 did King David despise the commandment of God in verse 9 when he did evil?

8.) – T. or. F. In 2 Kings 6:1-27 when the man disobeyed, was his family, have leprosy forever?

9.) – T. or. F. In Acts 2:37-42 did they ask Apostle's and Peter, men and brethren, what shall we do?

10.) – T. or. F. In Acts 9:1-21 did Saul change to Apostle Paul and so he taught, the same words, that Apostle Peter spoke in Acts 2:37-42.

11.) – T. or. F. In the whole book of Acts, did those Apostles obey and feed the church, the same way as in Acts 2:37-42 to the end?

12.) – T. or. F. In Romans 3:10 does it say, as it is written, there is none righteous, no not one?

13.) – T. or. F. In, Romans 11:13 did Apostle Paul say, I speak to you Gentiles, am I the Apostle of the Gentiles?

14.) – T. or. F. In Romans 14:10-12 does it say we shall all stand before the judgement seat of Christ?

15.) – T. or. F. In Acts 2:38 does it say, repent and be baptized every one of you in the name of Jesus Christ for the remission of sins?

16.) – T. or. F. In Philippians 2:9-12, If Jesus is our judge, should we all work out our own salvation with fear and trembling?

17.) – T. or. F. In James 2:19, 20 does it say the devils tremble, that they know one God, verse 20 But will thou know, O vain man, that faith without works is dead?

18.) – T. or. F. In 1 Peter 3:21 does it say even baptism does now save us?

19.) – T. or. F. In John 3:3-5 did Jesus say, we must be born again of the water and Spirit?

20.) – T. or. F. In Acts 1:4-8 and 13-15 and 2:1-42 did those 120 plus 3,000 more souls obey the Apostles, plus Peter's words, and got baptized in Jesus' lovely name?

21.) – T. or. F. In Acts 19:1-8 did Apostle Paul rebaptize them, even after, they were all once, baptized in John's baptism, did he also lay his hands on them, for them to receive the Holy Ghost, by them speaking in tongues?

22.) – T. or. F. In Acts 26:14-28 did King Agrippa know and believe the truth, and did he say almost thou persuades me to be a Christian?

23.) – T. or. F. Since you believe the Apostles, do you want to obey the Apostles true born again doctrine, and be ready for Jesus' great day on the clouds with those first saints and those who are asleep in Jesus, also those true born again Christians?

Chapter 14

Eternal Life Insurance

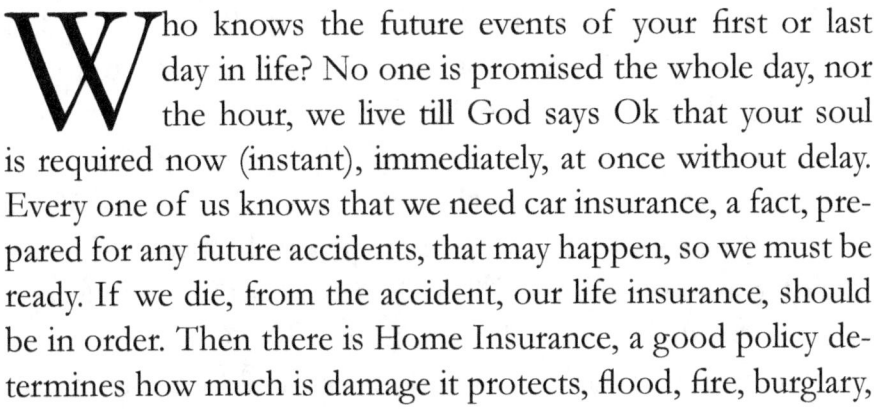

Who knows the future events of your first or last day in life? No one is promised the whole day, nor the hour, we live till God says Ok that your soul is required now (instant), immediately, at once without delay. Every one of us knows that we need car insurance, a fact, prepared for any future accidents, that may happen, so we must be ready. If we die, from the accident, our life insurance, should be in order. Then there is Home Insurance, a good policy determines how much is damage it protects, flood, fire, burglary, vandalism, was done to our homes.

So we should get a good smoke detector, with the best sounding alarm. We don't need no used car, nor house, or a second hand special. It's a fact, our families life is very dear to all of us, get the best possibly insurance, and cars, that your money can buy, for your protection. Now let us talk about a boat, how big, how new, just a small motor or a large motor, do you want to get halfway to your destination. Eternal life is a destination, the most important (journey) you will ever finish. Moses was the first one Jesus spoke about, in Luke 16:19-31 Abraham said, son your brothers, they have Moses and the prophets, let them hear them. Finished. Now in today time we have those – 12 Disciples, the Apostles, Jesus' words in red print, the books of Acts, Apostle Paul's words and his warning (alarms) about the devil's tricky, false doctrines, how he deceived, Adam and Eve, from his tricky words, how he deceives the world. The Apostle's doctrine is the Early First Church True Doctrine, only. Those Apostles preached and died for Jesus' name baptism. Then speaking in Tongues, as they all 120, plus 3,000 others, received the same (Holy Ghost gift filling.) The Journey started there and today, Apostolic, Apostle's true Doctrine is being preached, to the final destination, all man kinds finish (journey) till the last day of time. The Lord said in John3:1-7 verse 7 Marvel not that I said unto thee, ye (must) a command, requirement, obligation, or necessity. Jesus' own words. Saint Peter's words in Acts 2:37 They asked Peter and the rest of Apostles men and brethren, what shall we do? Verse 38 then Peter said unto them, repent, and be baptized every one of you in the name of (Jesus Christ) for the remission of sins, and ye shall receive the gift of the Holy Ghost. Verse 39 For the promise is unto you, and to your children, and to (all) that (a far off) even as many as the Lord God shall call. That was and is today, our one and only Doctrine, true Eternal Life Insurance, it doesn't cost a dime. Jesus payed the full price, you accept Apostle's (Apostolic Church's) Doctrine or second death, outside the New Jerusalem.

The Apostle Paul was persecuting (Jesus) the Churches Apostles. Then one day, Jesus blinded (Saul) or Paul, form a light, from heaven. Acts 9:1-6 And he (Saul) before named

JESUS' APOSTLES - TRUE BORN AGAIN DOCTRINE

Apostle Paul, trembling and astonished said, Lord, what wilt thou have me to do? And the Lord said unto him. Arise, and go into the City, and it shall be told thee what thou (must) command to do. Read Chapter Acts 9:1-43 How Apostle Paul and Apostle Peter, after they both was (converted) transformed into (Apostolic) Apostle's true Doctrine, how they turned, the First Original Church, into many true Christians. Apostle Paul, wasn't a believer till (Jesus) blinded him, then had someone tell him, what he must do, a (command) (order) just like in Acts 2:37 verse 37 they asked the Apostles, men and brethren, what shall we do?

Jesus said in John 3:3-5 except a man be born of water and of the Spirit, he cannot enter into the Kingdom of god. Yes, Apostle Peter told those men and brethren what they (must) was command to do. 3,000 souls that day, plus those 120 first received the Holy Ghost, spoke in tongues and was baptized in Jesus' lovely name, Apostle's doctrine. 1 Timothy 4:16 take heed unto thyself, and to the Doctrine; continue in them: for in doing this thou shalt save thyself, and them that hear thee. Ephesians 4:30 And grieve not the Holy Spirit of God, whereby ye are (sealed) guarantee (his fate) raised, safety, unto the day of redemption, coming of the Lord.

The (Acts) Book of Apostles, Apostle Paul wrote all these Books, started in Acts Book to Hebrews, Paul warded all of us, about how false Apostles, is coming, after his work was finished and the works of all those Apostles, next in the Council of Nicea, 325 AD The Emperor Constantine, their own Encyclopedia claims that Tertullian coined the term (Trinity). He and Justin Martyr, along with Augustine, decided to change (Jesus' name) in Baptism, into (Trinity) he Constantine rebaptized his entire army, in the words (Father, Son and Holy Ghost). He advised all that were baptized in Jesus' name, to be rebaptized the same way. This, of course, is contrary (opposite) to the Original Churches baptism. Sadly, the tragic part of all, that most churches today, major churches have taught that changed baptism. Yes, they still preach in Jesus' lovely name, cast out demons, in Jesus' lovely name. But, sadly, Jesus' name for remission of sins, was cast out. Jesus took those Early Original Apostle's sins away, in his name baptism. Apostle Peter said in Acts 2:38-42. This is for you, your children, even all that a far off, last day. Thank God, Apostle (Apostolic Churches) still obey those words, today.

Chapter -14- Eternal Life Insurance – Questions

True (T) or False (F)

1.) – T. or. F. In Revelation 1:3 Blessed is he that readeth, and they that hear the words of this prophecy, and keep those things which are written there in for the time is at hand.

2.) – T. or. F. In Matthew 20:28 Even as the son of man came not to be ministered unto, but to minister, and to give his life a ransom for many.

3.) – T. or. F. In Luke 7:29 And all the people heard him, and the publicans justified God, being baptized with the baptism of John.

4.) – T. or. F. In John 1:10 He was in the world, and the world was made by him, and the world knew him not.

5.) – T. or. F. In 1 Corinthians 15:1-9 verse 6 did five hundred brethren at once see Jesus, after he arose from the grave?

6.) – T. or. F. In 1 Corinthians 15:7 was Jesus seen of James; then of all the Apostles, after time of rising from the grave?

7.) – T. or. F. In 1 Corinthians 15:8 did Apostle Paul see Jesus?

8.) – T. or. F. In 2 Thessalonians 1:8 In flaming fire taking venge4ance on them that know not God, and that obey not the gospel of our Lord Jesus Christ.

9.) – T. or. F. In Hebrews 12:2 Looking unto Jesus the author and finisher of our faith; who for the joy that was set before him endured the cross, despising the shame, and is set down at the right hand of the throne of God.

10.) – T. or. F. In Revelation 20:6 Blessed and Holy is he that hath part in the first resurrection: on such the second death hath no power.

11.) – T. or. F. In Matthew 16:15-19 did Jesus give the keys of the kingdom of heaven, unto Peter and say, whatsoever thou shalt bind on earth, shall be bound in heaven?

12.) – T. or. F. In Luke 22:30-32 did Jesus tell Simon Peter, that after he was converted to strengthen his brethren and in his kingdom, he was also to set on thrones judging the twelve tribes of Israel?

13.) – T. or. F. In Acts 2:37-42 did Apostle Peter shake the keys for the kingdom of God, when he started to bind names on earth, and heaven?

14.) – T. or. F. In Romans 6:17 but ye have obeyed form the heart that form of doctrine which was delivered you.

15.) – T. or. F. In Acts 9:15-21 did Apostle Paul start to build the Church of God, after Jesus shines light on him, after he then was converted?

16.) – T. or. F. In Acts 26:13-19 There the Apostle Paul told King Agrippa how he was to bring the Gentiles out of darkness into the light, from the power of Satan unto God, verse 26-28 Almost a Christian?

17.) – T. or. F. In Luke 15:10 Will the angels of God, rejoice over one sinner (you) that repenteth and obey Acts 2:37-42?

18.) – T. or. F. In Acts 4:1-13 did Peter say there was no other name under heaven given among men, whereby we (must) be saved?

19.) – T. or. F. In Acts 5:25-32 did Peter and the rest of the Apostles say, we ought to obey God rather than men, verse 32 also did he say God would give the Holy Ghost to them that obey him?

20.) – T. or. F. In 1 Corinthians 6:1-3 did Apostle Paul say the Saints would judge the world and angels?

21.) – T. or. F. If the Apostles are to help Jesus judge the world and angels, are you bind on earth and heaven, as in Acts 2:37-42?

22.) – T. or. F. In the Book of Acts, did the Apostles, make sure they rebaptize from John's baptism, into Jesus' name baptism, and did the lay hands on them till they spoke in tongues, by Holy Ghost gift?

23.) – T. or. F. If our names isn't bind on earth or heaven, will we face the Revelation 20:5, 6, 11-15 the second death, cast into the lake of fire?

24.) – T. or. F. In Hebrews 10:22-31 is your true heart in full assurance of faith?

25.) – T. or. F. in 2 Corinthians 11:13-15 does Apostle Paul warn everybody about the devil old Satan deceitful working as an angel of light?

26.) – T. or. F. In Proverbs 3:5 Trust in the Lord with all thine heart and I cannot unto thine own understanding.

27.) – T. or. F. In John 11:23-25 did Jesus raise Lazarus from the dead after four days, did he also say, I am the resurrection and the life, 37-45 is Jesus' name on your baptism, for the resurrection day?

Chapter 15

Big T.V.'s Holy Ghost Filled Preachers

God filled you all with the Spirit, to draw all His sheep to Him. I watched each one of you on T.V., you spoke about the Power, after you received the Gift of tongues, that was promised to everyone. God gave this Spirit so you could be like those great early first Apostles, who baptized 3,000 souls on that Pentecost Day. Each week I see 10 times that amount in your big filled churches. Jesus said to Apostle Peter if you love me, feed my sheep, not once, nor twice, but 3 times, he told (command) Peter, that day. In Luke 22:31, 32 verse 32 But I have prayed for thee, that thy faith fail not; and when thou art converted, (transformed), strengthen thy brethren. Big preachers, now since you have the same Holy Ghost filling gift, you are converted, (transformed), will thy strengthen thy brethren. Let them know how you spoke in tongues, when you received the Holy Ghost. Acts 2:38-42 You have the power, just like Apostle Peter and those 120 others, plus those 3,000 souls, that was baptized in Jesus' lovely name,

Peter said, it your gift, your children, and to all, even those who are a far off, 2,000 years later, and Apostolic Churches still same doctrine. Apostle Peter rebaptized those 120, plus 3,000 souls in Jesus' lovely name.

Just like Apostle Paul in, Acts 19:1-6 5 When they heard this, they were baptized in the name of the Lord Jesus. 6 And when Paul had laid his hands upon them, the Holy Ghost (gift) came on them; and they spake with tongues. Acts 8:9-19 Simon the (sorcery) verse 13 Then Simon himself believed also, when he was baptized in the name of Jesus. Yes, he saw others get the Holy Ghost gift. He didn't receive the gift, he saw how Peter laying hands on them to get the Holy Ghost, Simon the (sorcery) wanted to buy this power, so he could lay hands on who so ever he wanted, because of this, he and his money would perish. Big T.V. Preachers, I say this with all respect, do you believe the Bible is truth. Apostle Paul wrote these (Acts) of Saint Peter, of all those Apostles, plus, his very own (convert) transform, change from a (persecutor) of the First Original Upper Room true Apostle's Doctrine Church, to all mankind. Who will baptize in Jesus' lovely name? Who will lay hands on Brothers and sisters, to they get the gift of the Spirit, just like Saint Peter, and Apostle Paul and 120 plus 3,000 souls, even these far off days, as each one of your preachers that received the Holy Ghost tongue speaking gift, this day. They laid the foundation for us, Moses, prophets, Apostles and Jesus Christ himself the chief corner stone.

It has been 1 year, since I wrote letters to your Churches, I never did got, no letter back, you might think, how could a man in Prison teach us anything about being born again by water and Spirit. Well Moses wrote the first five books, started in Genesis, Exodus, Leviticus, Numbers, and Deuteronomy, he once was a murderer, look how God changed his life. King David wrote a few books in the Old Testament, well we all know his story, but after he changed, God said King David was a man after God's own heart. Jonah, Jonah ran from God, he disobeyed God's command to warn Nineveh, but, look at the Big Fish story in the Bible, how he did warn Nineveh and wasn't destroyed. Now let's go to the New Testament, Matthew 26:69-75 Then Peter denied with an oath 3 times, I never known that man. 74 Then began he to curse and to swear, saying, I know not the man. And immediately the cock crowed. Jesus had warned Peter, how the old devil would sift him like wheat. God lets the devil shifts us all like wheat, he started with Adam and Eve, look how he did Moses, King David, Jacob's ladder, finished just fine. We all know the Bible's history, how we all fall short of the Glory. Look at Saint Peter's whole life, Jesus gave him the keys to the kingdom of God, in Matthew 16:15-19 verse 19 and I will give unto thee the keys of the kingdom of heaven: and whatsoever thou shalt bind on earth shall be bound in heaven; and whatsoever thou loose on earth shall be loosed in heaven. We see here that Jesus gave Apostles a command to build His church, Apostle Peter started to bind on earth and heaven, the Day of Pentecost, Acts 2:14. But Peter, standing up with the eleven, (Apostles) lifted up his voice, and said unto them, Ye men of Judea, and all ye that dwell at Jerusalem, be this known unto you, and hearken (listen or hear or heed) to my words. 14-42 37 they said unto Peter and the rest of the Apostles, what shall we do? Now Peter was (converted) changed, transformed, by the Holy Ghost filling, after he and the Apostles, received the speaking in tongues, Power Gift to believers. 3,000 souls, saw and believed Peter's true Doctrine Words that day. They are was bind on earth and heaven, I'm sure some didn't believe or get bind on heart or heaven that Pentecost day, but they heard the keys of heaven, words.

Apostle Peter in the end turned out fit for the kingdom of heaven. Apostle Paul, in due time, started rattle those keys to those baptized in John's baptism. Just look how he told King Agrippa, I know you believest thou the prophets? I know thou believest. Acts 26:14-29 28 Then Agrippa said unto Paul, Almost thou persuades me to be a Christian. 29 And Paul said, I would to God, that not only thou, but also all that hear me this day, were both almost, and all together such as I am, except these bonds. Almost, ho, how said they almost was converted that sad day.

Chapter -15- Big – T.V.'s – Holy Ghost Filled Preachers

Questions – True (T) or False (F)

1.) – T. or. F. In Jonah 1:1-3 did Jonah obey the command of the Lord?

2.) – T. or. F. In John 21:9-17 did Jesus tell Peter three times, feed my sheep?

3.) – T. or. F. In Luke 22:29-32 Did Jesus tell Peter, When thou art converted, strengthen they brethren?

4.) – T. or. F. In Matthew 5:13-15 did Jesus say let your light shine, and don't hide it under a bushel?

5.) – T. or. F. In Acts 2:1-4 did you big preachers speak in tongues just like those 120 did, when they received the Holy Ghost?

6.) – T. or. F. In Acts 10:1-8 Apostle Paul asked those, have you received the Holy Ghost since you believed, now Big Show Preachers have you asked your churches, if they received the Holy Ghost, like you did when you believed, did you lay hands on church members, so they might?

7.) – T. or. F. In Acts 2:37-42 did Apostle Peter say it was for all those, their children, and even for all who are a far off?

8.) – T. or. F. In the Book of Acts, did all those Apostles baptize the brothers and sisters in Jesus' lovely name for the remission of sins?

9.) – T. or. F. In Acts 2:42 did they continue in the Apostle's true doctrine?

10.) – T. or. F. In Acts 10:34 Then Peter opened his mouth, and said, of a truth I perceive that god is no respecter of persons?

11.) – T. or. F. In Acts 10:41-48 did they speak in tongues when they received the Holy Ghost, then he commanded to be rebaptized in Jesus name?

12.) – T. or. F. In Acts 11:1-21 did they do the same as the beginning?

13.) – T. or. F. In Acts 13:22-47 did Apostle Paul and Barnabas say they was to be light of the Gentiles for salvation unto end of world?

14.) – T. or. F. In Romans 8:5-11 Is that Holy Spirit in you, the same Spirit, that raised Jesus form the dead?

15.) – T. or. F. In Romans 10:14-17 have you obey the gospel as in Acts 2:38-42?

16.) – T. or. F. In 1 Thessalonians 3:12, 13 are you ready for the coming of our Lord Jesus Christ with all his saints?

17.) – T. or. F. In 1 Thessalonians 4:13-18 The dead in Jesus shall rise first, then those which are alive and remain, shall rise to meet Jesus in the air to be with Jesus forever?

18.) – T. or. F. In 2 Thessalonians 2:1-12 who believed not the truth, as in the Apostle's Acts 2:37-42 and John 3:3-5?

19.) – T. or. F. In Timothy 2:4 Who will have all men to be saved, and to come unto the knowledge of the truth?

20.) – T. or. F. In James 2:20 But wilt thou know, O vain man, that faith without works is dead?

21.) – T. or. F. In 1 Peter 3:18-21 verse 18 but quickened by the Spirit and verse 21 the like figure where unto even baptism doth also now save us.

22.) – T. or. F. In 1 Corinthians 14:39 wherefore, covet to prophesy and forbid not to speak in tongues?

23.) – T. or. F. In Revelation 20:5-21 does it say we all will rise from the dead, the first resurrection shall rise to Jesus' calling in the cloud of glory, sadly the second resurrection is for the second death at judgement, the great white throne, for the lake of fire, second death?

24.) – T. or. F. In Acts 18:25 John's baptism, for repentance?

25.) – T. or. F. In Acts 19:1-7 Preachers are you still preaching John's baptism for repentance?

26.) – T. or. F. In Acts 2:37-42 and John 3:3-5 Born again of water and Spirit, same Doctrine truth as in Acts 19:1-7 Jesus' name, and baptized in Jesus' name and speaking in tongues as you are filled with the Holy Ghost Spirit, eternal life with those great Apostles and our Great Lord and Saviour Jesus Christ?

Chapter 16

Fire, After Water

In Zechariah 14:12 And this shall be the plague wherewith the Lord will smite all the people that have fought against Jerusalem: Their flesh shall consume away while they stand upon their feet, and their eyes shall consume away in their holes, and their tongue shall consume in their mouth. Please read and understand that the Day of the Lord is coming, where shall you be this day, Chapter 14 is telling (all) that the Rapture could happen (occur) take place, in a twinkle of an eye, if you miss (failure) to be in it. The world, what is left of it, will go to 7 years of very hard times. Read the Old and New Testament, we all know God's plan, He made a way for Noah in the Ark, the Flood washed all sins away. Those who didn't obey God's plan, was destroyed by water. 1 Peter 3:18-22 Jesus came and gave his life for them, us. All mankind, Adam to End time. In John 3:3-5 Jesus said (commanded) everyone to be born of water and Spirit. Matthew 28:18 And Jesus came and spake unto them, saying, all power is given unto me in heaven and earth. Matthew 16:17-19 Are you bind on earth and Heaven? Did you obey Jesus' command to be born of water and of the Spirit? Apostle Peter said in Acts 2:38-42 This was for them, their children and to (all) who are (a Far off) end time. From Day of Pentecost, till the last man or woman born. As you can (all) see there are many Churches, Apostle's Doctrine still going on, just like that (Original Church) started in Jerusalem, 33 AD in the Upper Room, those 120 plus 3,000 souls.

Acts 2:1-4 verse 3 And there appeared unto them (cloven tongues like as of fire), as the (Spirit) gave them utterance (voice, speech, speaking) (Power). Who has that (fire of tongues) (power) like those 120 Acts 1:12-16 Read this, that original church started that day in Jerusalem, Peter and disciples, with the mother of Jesus (Mary) and with the women, Apostle Peter had shaken the keys, started the (words) to the (true water and Spirit). Born again Salvation men and women got the (Spirit of Fire Tongues) plus 3,000 souls added. Which water and Fire do you want? Jesus' name water? Get that same Holy Ghost gift, like those who was truly born again of water and Spirit, they all were bind on Earth and Heaven that Pentecost Day. Brothers and sisters, please, please don't miss the Rapture, you don't want yourself, or your family, nor Church members to fail the Fire Death. After that first death, (Revelation 20:6) second death 11-15 second death, for those not written in the Book of Life. Bind on earth and Heaven's books. Don't be loosed on Earth and Heaven's Book. Please brothers and sisters, check the Bible, Acts 2:38-42, John 3:3-5, Jesus' name Baptism.

We can read again in Old Testament, 2 Kings 5:1-16 7 times in water. In Acts 2:38-42 They rebaptized them the second time, first was John's baptism. Then in Acts 19:1-6 Paul baptized all twelve of them in Jesus' lovely name. The New Testament, was written by a once nonbeliever, Paul. Please Read, 1 Corinthians 1:2 Apostle was wrote to the Church of God, Saints, we was written to the Church, those who were already born again, if he called them Saints or Brethren, he was warning them all, not to fall back nor teach any other (Doctrine) 1st Timothy 1:3 that they teach no other (Doctrine.) Hebrews 5:9, 6:1-2 They laid the foundation for us (all).

If Apostle's laid the Original Church Foundation that day, and said unto the coming of the Lord, Jesus' day, where are your names now? Book of Life, like those 120 plus 3,000 souls, plus (all) who follow Saint Peter's (keys) words of Life, Books of life, chose this Day, who you obey, Jesus and His Apostles, or Blind leading the Blind. That old devil, doesn't want (all) to be in the Book of Life, Adam and Eve, found out first, death has came on us (all) don't let that second death happen to you. When we say, yes I believe the whole Bible truth, then believe Acts 2:38-42 and John 3:3-5 It wasn't for them only, Saint Peter's words is and was for them, their children, and to (all) who are (a far off) end times.

Please check the Bible, website, see when the original Church started. Check when your church started, Apostolic Churches follow Apostle Peter's true salvation, same doctrine 2,000 years now, Add your name and family in the Book of Life in Earth and Heaven, first death is bad enough, don't let that old devil keep you in darkness, darkness, come to light and life. Brothers and sisters, do you know that there is no other name in or under heaven, whereby we (must) commanded to be saved by Jesus' name baptism. The Holy Ghost is Fire and Life, we all must be born of water and Spirit. Ask Apostolic Preachers, your call can help save you, your family, church.

Glory to Glory, be in the Rapture, you don't want no part of the great 7 year tribulation. It's bad enough in this world now, just think when the Saint and churches, and Holy Ghost leaves, no power on Earth will stop those final end times, oh how I sorrow for those that didn't make the Rapture moment, the Great White Throne, small and great will stay there. I can only warn you like Moses, Prophets, Jesus, Apostles, and all who teach God's truth. Watch the news, Gospel is already spread in all the world, knowledge is increased, 2,000 years ago. How long will God delay His coming in clouds. Workout your own salvation with fear and trembling. Philippians 2:12

13.) – T. or. F. In John 3:3-10 did Jesus tell the teacher (Preacher) Nicodemus, how do you not know these things about water and Spirit?

14.) – T. or. F. In Romans 10:13-21 are you the branch of the tree like those Apostles brought the born again true gospel to Acts 2:37-42 and John 3:3-5 down to the end of time, for every nation to hear?

15.) – T. or. F. What can wash away my sins, nothing but the blood of Jesus, as in Acts 2:38 baptized in Jesus' name for the remission of sins?

16.) – T. or. F. In Acts 13:43-52 did Apostle Paul and Barnabas say the Lord commanded us to be a light to the Gentiles for Salvation, even to the ends of the earth?

17.) – T. or. F. In Acts 12:1-25 did Peter and the Apostles keep preaching then return to Jerusalem?

18.) – T. or. F. In Acts 22:10-16 And now why tarriest thou? Arise, and be baptized, and wash away thy sins, calling on the name of the Lord.

19.) – T. or. F. In Romans 11:13 For I speak to you Gentiles, inasmuch as I am the Apostle of the Gentiles, I magnify mine office

20.) – T. or. F. In 1 Corinthians 2:10 But God has reveal them unto us by his (Spirit): For the Spirit searcheth all things, yea the deep things of God.

Conclusion

The hour is slowly about to the coming of Lord Jesus. We are a Twinkle of an Eye away from Eternity. We don't have a second chance for our life on Earth. God gives us all, Prophets, Moses, those Apostles and all the signs of knowledge, so fast these last years in time. A thousand years is like a day to God, so as all these days He gave Mankind, it's a blessing, we must be born again, for the kingdom, read those Revelation's chapters, see how wonderful our New Earth and Home shall ever be. God doesn't want no one to die that second death, he took our First Death on that Old Rugged Cross, for our sins, all sins. John the Baptist, Preached and Baptized all for repentance, with water, but he said Jesus would baptize with the Holy Ghost and Fire, Spirit, the water, next the Spirit. Jesus gave His disciples the Holy Ghost in Matthew 10:1-19. There they were called, 12 Apostles, first Simon, is called Peter. If we say we all believe those Apostles, then we all must obey those

Saints, they started at Jerusalem, waited on the Promise of the Father, John baptized with water, but ye shall be baptized with the Holy Ghost. Acts 1:1-26 waited. Acts 2:1-42 They got the Holy Ghost Promise, then got baptized again, this time not by John the Baptist, but by the Apostle's baptism, in the name of Jesus Christ for the (remission)(pardon) for sins. Apostle Peter said this is for you your children and all who are a far off, as many as God calls. Yes, a thousand years to God it's like 1 day, we now had 2 thousand years, we had 2 days, time is latter days now. Watch the news, US President told North Korea, you're starting the Battle of Armageddon, if you keep things going with missiles. These days a twinkle of an eye, the battle could start any second of time. So you must be ready to go, before the great 7 year Tribulation Days God is ready for all to be born again, Apostle's Doctrine.

About the Author

I'm just a Born-Again Brother that Jesus changed to bring light, as Apostle Paul started, to all the world, even to us, who are afar off.

Come to the light while there is time. Soon this world shall end. Be with the 120 saints, plus 3,000 and all that obey John 3:3-5 and ACTS 2:37-42. The church that Jesus built on Pentecost Day, is still calling us all. Get your name in the book of LIFE, not second death. Jesus said, I am the way, the truth and life. Not just repent. John already had them Baptized for repentance. So, don't stop, get re-baptized in Jesus' name, and speak in tongues as ye receive the Holy Ghost, for all, far off days.

From Brother Clarke Smith
\# 273-624
MCTC-EHU
18800 Roxbury Road
Hagerstown, Maryland 21746

www.ingramcontent.com/pod-product-compliance
Lightning Source LLC
Chambersburg PA
CBHW071902070526
44583CB00016B/1808